# The Conquest of FEAR

M. F. Graham, M.D.

BROADMAN PRESS
Nashville, Tennessee

*1696*

## Dedication

To my very dear friend in Christ,
Reverend Jack B. Rittelmeyer,
without whose prayers this book
in all likelihood
would never have been written

"The effectual fervent prayer
of a righteous man availeth much"
(James 5:16)

*"The divine mystery is absolute,
while nothing in science can be so viewed."*
*Irvine H. Page, M.D.*

# Preface

The libraries of this world are replete with volume upon volume about fear—that awesome "last of ills" which, in one or another form, hounds man so inexorably and inevitably as he wends his way through life. This fact in itself bespeaks the complexity, as well as the enormity, of fear, and perhaps also strives to say something about man's "fear of fear," which has led to all sorts of human experience—some constructive, some destructive; some good, some bad—but all with one motive: the conquest of fear.

Fear is a two-edged sword. Out of perspective, it is a devil which drives man to destruction. Seen in its true light, it is a guardian angel. Like darkness and light, sometimes black, sometimes white, it permeates the thought of man in one or another shade of grey, is warp and woof of his starkest hours and, yet again, his smoothest seas.

To begin with, I should clearly point out that this volume is not a work of medicine, although it alludes to the work of many scientists, chiefly medical. Neither is it, although it leans upon faith, a book on "religion," for I have no faith in "religion." Rather, it is an effort to point out how one realm of medical science has, in my own life, been wedded to a personal faith in Jesus Christ toward the conquest of fear, the worst kind of fear, the fear of death.

With the mention of the name of Jesus Christ, I am well aware that I stand to lose a large portion of my potential readers, a regrettable but calculated risk, for without him this book would never—in fact, could never—have been written. To give him less than a place of supreme prominence within these pages would be to do likewise with him in my life; with him who has meant the difference to me between life and death, both temporal and eternal.

In short, it is not my avowed purpose to produce a bestseller. It is my purpose to tell a story—a story about one man as it really happened, outside him and inside, a man who never really learned how to live until brought face to face with death and was caught up in the paralyzing, stultifying, cold, clammy grip of fear! And from the telling of this story, God being my helper, is my devout hope that others may make similar discoveries to the one I have made, and in so doing begin living anew, whether or not those others are victims of physical disease. For fear is no respecter of one's physical status. And its conquest need not await some terrifying moment when one stands looking into the gaping maw of his own grave.

The conquest of fear opens doors that will remain forever closed to those who cower and cringe in the grip of this devastating emotion. And he who at an early age puts fear in its proper perspective, who does not wait for some infirmity to touch him, will have taken his first giant stride toward confident living. And, paradoxically and ironically, confident living hinges on confident death.

It is therefore not the purpose of this text to present in depth scientific or theological material, to debate side issues, or to refute rebuttals, but rather to present an experience and the results of that experience, so that the reader may investigate the reference material for himself, and put to test in his own life the principles formulated herein, thus to answer for himself the question which naturally arises: In the fiery crucible of life, *do these principles really work?*

In acting on the experience of one man, herein related, it is hoped that others may utilize guideposts derived from the best light that medical science has uncovered to date, and may also find that any principle of life, however thrilling and rewarding, is incomplete if God be left out. In so doing it is hoped that the reader also may discover that there *is* a mode of living which leaves nothing to be desired, either here or hereafter.

This book represents, then, an amalgamation of the love and the laws of God, as expressed and personified by his Son, Jesus Christ, with what is known currently in a particular realm of medicine about a particular disease—coronary ("heart attack") disease. However, the principles set forth apply to other illnesses as well; in fact, to preventive medicine in general. The book concerns itself primarily with the living of life—i.e., the application of principle —and the facts presented, the knowledge utilized, are but means rather than ends in themselves.

Such pragmatism doubtless stems in large measure from my being a practitioner of medicine rather than a theorist, a fact that makes me something of an artist as well as a scientist, since the practice of medicine is at once an art and a science.

Similar principle applies to the spiritual aspect of this writing. Not being a theologian, I have no dogma to defend. I am committed to no creed or credo. I have tried, on the personal field of battle, and in the same cold light that I have prescribed for others an injection for some deadly microbe, the Person that is Jesus Christ. I have not found him wanting!

Although this book grew out of the life experience of one man in his desperate encounter with fear, and it alludes to certain technical aspects of this encounter, it reflects the work and the experience of many men in many fields. Where appropriate, references are indicated and presented in bibliographic form at the end of the book, so that those so inclined may pursue the lines of thought to their more exhaustive beginnings and endings.

It is hoped that many of the millions whose heads lie uneasy beneath the Damoclean sword of coronary heart disease or other life-palling disease, as well as millions whose lives are yet unshadowed by physical illness, may read this small volume and go away with a lease on life—nay, a new life—which is precisely what one derives from the true conquest of fear.

# Table of Contents

# CHAPTER I

# Black Friday

The day is past, and yet I saw no sun;
And now I live, and now my life is done.
Tichborne

It was on a letter-perfect, sunny Friday afternoon. I shall never forget it. I sat opposite the cardiologist to whom my own physician had referred me because of some questionably abnormal T-waves in my electrocardiogram (EKG). On a view-box behind the heart specialist X-Rays cast their contrasting shadows, and on the desk before him lay a long strip of paper with an undulating line down its middle, a freshly-traced EKG. I felt a wee bit fatigued, but pleasantly so, from three sets of tennis singles which I had played just before coming to see him. I expected the best, that the questionable EKG tracing which my own physician had found on routine physical examination was but a physiologic variation of normal, just as he had told me it probably was and I had been only too willing to believe.

The cardiologist reared back in his chair, adjusted his glasses, and fixed his unswerving gaze on me. "You have coronary disease, I'm afraid."

At first the words hung limply in mid-air, too barefaced, too plain to comprehend. Then, quickly, engulfing me like a great net, they descended on me and drug me down into an abysmally lonely sea in which I groped, helplessly, for a life jacket.

"You're sure?"

He nodded a stern affirmative.

From out of the depths of that stormy sea in which I suddenly floundered, I argued vehemently. I fired my *ifs, ands,* and *buts* like broadside salvos at a pirate frigate. But the heart specialist remained steadfast in his conviction. Vaguely I recall some of the things he recommended: "Get plenty of rest." "Cut down on your work." "If you play tennis, play doubles." "Stay with a low fat, low cholesterol diet."

Haplessly, hopelessly, I fought back like a trapped animal. "But I can't afford more time off. And I don't like doubles tennis. And low fat diets are about as tasty as grass on a spinach leaf."

He only knitted his brows disapprovingly at my protestations and stuck by his guns.

This man had hit me everywhere I lived, but he wasn't through. He gave me a pocketful of vasodilator pills (samples) and told me to take one every so often. This was medication whose pharmacologic action was to dilate the coronary arteries that feed the heart, in an effort to get more blood to heart muscle with a compromised blood supply.

Then came the clincher, the last of the coffin nails: "And keep some demerol on hand, just in case." Demerol is a powerful narcotic, and the implication of his recommendation was obvious. It was comparable to saying: "A heart attack could hit you any time now." Might as well tell a man he is sitting on a keg of gunpowder that could explode at any moment; that the fuse was lit and no one knew how long it was! I was stunned, poleaxed, and as I at length wobble-legged out of his office and down the long, long stairs, a shaft of sunlight that beamed through a window swam crazily through my tears.

As I emerged into the sunlight again, sunlight whose warmth and brilliance had filled me with thoughts of life but an hour or so before, I was no longer aware of the blue and green and gold afternoon so resplendent in its fall array. Rather, I was full of the thoughts of death, and there was all about me only a shadowy and menacing blackness, emblematic of the darkness within.

Indeed, I no longer was the same man. Suddenly I wasn't a young 42 any more. Suddenly I couldn't do the things I always had done for years and years and forever. Suddenly I was very old. Suddenly I was a cripple, a cardiac cripple. The afternoon had begun with life as my infinite friend. It had ended with death as my imminent enemy. When I had ascended those stairs I had been full of the feel of life: confident, certain of tomorrow, captain of my own destiny. Now, descending, I was seized with a bottomless hopelessness, a dank and dismal and choking despair, and a dreadful mental and physical paresis such as can stem only from the abyss of the unknown, from the womb of fear.

Zombie-like, I got into my sporty, chromed-up automobile and headed home. But on arrival I did not, as was customary, seek out my wife or my two little boys. Rather, with great stealth, I crept to my bedroom, cringing like a whipped cur, not feeling that I belonged with the living and the well.

In a moment my wife came in. She sensed my despair, put her arms about me, and probed my problem. I remember few of the details I related, but I do recall telling her one thing. "It's funny, Wife," I said, "but the first automobile I ever owned, when I was only twenty, was a black one. It's strange, isn't it, that the last one, the one I have now, is also black. You know, all the others have been some other color."

She tried to laugh, as though to deride my sobriety and thereby banish my dejection, but it was a feeble effort, as was her half-hearted remark meant to bolster my sagging spirits: "You'll outlive us all!" Her words in that moment irritated me. I fact, I thought them worse than none at all, and I asked to be alone. Understandingly, she complied with my request.

Alone again, I unloosed a flood of tears that had been dammed up for an hour or so. I disliked crying. It wasn't what a man should do, I thought. But I was at that moment only half a man who wouldn't be around too much longer, anyhow. I leaned forward in my chair, cradled my head between my arms, and the tears came until there were no more. In that time I knew why men commit suicide. When a man teeters on the edge of a precipice, and there are no routes of escape, sometimes he jumps—or simply falls.

The tug on my shoulder was gentle, almost apologetic, and in the semi-darkness of the room I raised my head and looked into the beautiful face of my three-year-old boy.

"Daddy, come play with me," he said.

I clasped him to me and he melted into my arms, sensing, it seemed, my deep despair. And then the four-year old came and joined the circle of my arms. I felt their hearts pounding against my very own. Their small, young hearts against this old and deci-mated thing inside my chest. Their strong hearts against my weak one. Their healthy hearts against my disease-ridden one.

*Dear God,* I thought, *if only I could spare them an hour like this! Dear God,* I prayed, *spare me, for yet a little while, for these two boys.*

Years later, I know that God answered that prayer, for out of the wet depths of my stark fear and depression I rose up, like a spaniel leaving a dank and dismal pond, shook off the dampness, and resolved—for the moment, at least—to acquit myself like a man.

"O.K.," I smiled, "let's play." .

We played, my boys and I, and in the laughter that followed a new and God-given strength welled up within me. I began to ask what I could best do with what remained of my life. From this nidus of hope was to emerge a program which, had I begun it decades before when I was the age of my boys, would have made it far more likely that this infamous day at least would have been delayed for many years.

So with the prayer that God would guide me and that, be it his will, I might be with these dear boys into their young manhood (for my own father had died when I was only twelve and I knew the foreboding problems of orphanhood), I seized upon the for-ward look. Eagerly I began the solution of my paramount problem: how to make the most of life with a crippled heart. The quest was to lead me to medical libraries, far and wide medical meetings relating to the problem, and to communication with people top-notch in their fields.

Moreover, it was again to lead me to my knees before God. It was to replace concern about bank accounts, automobiles, houses, things, and "stuff," with concern about life—the living of the here and now, and the preparation for the life to come. It was once again to reset the focus of my life to where it had been decades before; it was to change it from man and time to God and eternity. It was to lead to a way of life which, had I but known it, was what I had been in search of for lo these many years, a way which, when all is said and done, is the better way under any circumstance—heart disease, any disease, or no disease. It was to formulate a plan which, put into action as early in life as possible and maintained throughout, has rewards beyond the fondest dreams of any man, both here and hereafter. Thus was this black Friday to become bright Friday, for it was the will of God.

# CHAPTER II

# A Thief Called Fear

My hair is grey, but not with years,
Nor grew it white
In a single night,
As men's have grown from sudden fears.
Byron

In the preceding chapter I intimated that in one fleeting moment, spurred on by the presence of my two young boys, I decided to acquit myself as a man, and that was the end of the entire dilemma. Would that it had been that easy! It was, to tell the truth, far from easy. For the courage of the moment, born of the presence of my own flesh and blood, gave way that very night to the despair of futility. Driven by a relentless fear, I was not, for a time, my own.

The state of precarious uncertainty in which the cardiologist's dire pronouncement had placed me created a state of semi-shock of considerable mental confusion. As Burke so aptly put it: "No passion so effectually robs the mind of all its powers of acting and reasoning as fear."

This is not to say that I was totally immobilized, for with some strength born not of myself (it must have been of the grace of God), I still managed to carry on my work and a modicum of former activities. I even managed a fairly respectable front when around others.

It was when I was alone that the walls came tumbling down around me and the roof caved in. I came to dread the endless nights, wondering when I lay down to "rest" if I should be permitted to see another dawn. And even as I carried on my daily activities I did so with a great weight hung about my neck like a dread

16

albatross. Succinctly, life simply was no good.

There were times when I contemplated self-destruction. But again, something—no, Someone—restrained me; Someone beyond flesh and blood. For as much as I loved and wanted to be with my family, I came to feel that I was but a burden and a threat to their happiness. Much of the "fun" and spontaneity had gone from being together, for tomorrow was now such an uncertain thing. Almost as much as death, I dreaded the crippling effect of a bad heart attack that reduces a man, though still living, to a shackled manni-kin of his former self, more dead than alive. Such attitudes could not be concealed, I knew, and they were deadly to the happiness of my loved ones.

I realized that I could not go on living under the spell of fear. I further realized that in the end either fear would destroy me or I would master it. There was no middle ground. Quite by chance (or was it?) in my evening reading I came across an article, very forcefully written, to the effect that a given fear must be mastered by meeting it on its own ground, by standing up to it and slugging it out toe to toe. Somehow this thought, by its appearance in print, I suppose (though it was a thought I had mulled over many times), crystallized my thinking. It served in much the same fashion that a crystalline speck, dropped into a supersaturated solution of itself, affords a nidus about which the excess solute precipitates. It was the spark that started the clearing of a muddled mind.

It was reasonable from the start that the more one could learn about his fear the less menacing it might become. Such has been the case. I think that God made it so with me. In fact, I believe that each step of my path—from newspaper clippings on up or down the scale of learning about my plight—has been directed by God. If this seems naive, so be it, but I pray that you finish my story before you draw any final conclusions.

To begin with, I wanted to know more about fear itself. What is it? Why is it? Where is it? and so on. Certain things about it are obvious, of course—the sweaty palms, the tense muscles, the dilated pupils, the elevated blood pressure, the rapid pulse, the increased respiratory rate—all physiologic manifestations of fear. Then there was the mental turmoil, the confusion, the depression, the panic that are fear's footprints in the mind. And finally, there was the utter loneliness and dejection, the feeling of abandonment, that represented a man cut off from all hope. This was fear's worst attribute, its ability to separate a man from reality, to render him insensate to God's promises, such as: "I will never leave thee, nor forsake thee" (Heb. 13:5); "Fear thou not; for I am with thee: be not dismayed; for I am thy God" (Isa. 41:10); "There is no fear in love; but perfect love casteth out fear" (1 John 4:18).

It would be futile and purpose-defeating, even if space permitted, here to attempt to launch into anything like a comprehensive treatise on fear. I shall therefore no more than outline certain of its properties and qualifications, and that but to lay some groundwork for what is to follow.

Webster defines fear as a distressing emotion aroused by impending pain, danger, evil, etc., whether real or imaginary. In certain of its dimensions fear is synonymous with anxiety, which in turn begets tension, about which a great deal more is to be said later in connection with factors operative in the causation of heart attacks.

Fear has been described in various writings down through the centuries as everything from a thief to a murderer. Who could deny that it is any and all of these things—and more. A thief and a murderer, yes. But also a liar, a cheat, and a cruel and unrelenting antagonist of reason and soundness of mind. Fear is, in fact, an unholy taskmaster. "For God hath not given us the spirit of fear; but of power, and of love, and of a sound mind" (2 Tim. 1:7).

Donne, in his "Hymn to God the Father," speaks of his sin of fear. Shakespeare, in "Antony and Cleopatra," points out that "in time we hate that which we often fear." According to Tennyson, fear, like an axeman, is capable of sundering faith and form ("In Memoriam"). When all is said and done, fear is a "thing" that defies description. It is a sweaty-palmed, icy-eyed, breathless, shadowy, and cruel cutthroat, bereft of reason, shorn of logic, and foreign to faith in the Lord Jesus Christ.

The dimensions which fear possesses are those of depth (intensity), length (duration), and breadth (whether real—i.e., broad-based—or imaginary). Its relativity in time and circumstance is a fourth dimension which may in large measure alter the other three. For example, a fatal disease in a very old person may produce a fear lacking the depth which the same disease would produce in a young person.

Fear is as ubiquitous as life itself, and no thinking man has ever escaped its clutches entirely. That man who says he never has been afraid is either a moron or a liar. I have talked with any number of men who would be classified as brave by all human standards: men awarded decorations for bravery in battle, some in the air, some in the trenches, some in bunkers—and I have yet to find one who would deny that at one or another time, faced with danger, he experienced fear.

(And here I might interject that there is nothing wrong with being afraid. The emotion is intensely human. But to be mastered by fear: that is the sin, the crime, the horror. For some bravery comes easy; a factor determined in some measure by genetics, in part by early environment. For others, it comes with great effort.)

The effects of fear are variable. It can kill outright. It is well-documented, for example, that in certain primitive tribes a spell of death, when cast by the witch doctor upon one who has trespassed tribal law, inevitably results in the death of the bewitched, albeit slowly, as surely as if beheaded. Jesus Christ said that in the last days of this age men's hearts would fail them for fear. But we need not wait until then to see this happen. Medical records are full of incidents wherein fatal heart attacks have been precipitated by some great fear.

Fear can paralyze. I recall one instance of a young man who, fearful of losing his sweetheart following a violent quarrel, fell to the sidewalk in front of her house, and when brought to the hospital was found to be completely paralyzed and insensate from the waist down—a so-called conversion hysteria.

Fear can convulse. There was the young nurse who, quite regularly following a lover's quarrel, filled with the fear of losing her prospective mate, would hyperventilate and be thrown into a convulsive state.

Fear can immobilize. I recall the report of an incident wherein an auto containing two men stalled on a railroad track with a train bearing down upon the crossing. One man jumped out forthwith, but the other was too terrified to move. He was yanked out of the jaws of death by his friend in just the nick of time.

Fear incapacitates. Fear of a heart attack will put a once active man in his rocking chair, a fact documented again and again and again, and one which is at the center of our present story.

Need we go on? The point is clear. Though we cannot see fear *per se,* we can see all too readily its kaleidoscopic effects upon our fellow beings. Not a day of medical practice passes but what I see fear many times in a multitude of forms. The same can be said by anyone who takes the trouble to look for it.

One must quite naturally ask the *why* of the emotion of fear. And when fear is seen to have a protective function, at least in a physical sense, it becomes clear that fear is not altogether a bad thing at all. Unpleasant, yes. And sometimes with painful consequences. But not always evil.

The little infant, with an innate fear only of falling and of loud noises, soon learns as he passes through childhood, that fire, for example, is painful if he puts his hand in it. He comes to respect fire, to fear it healthfully. Thus does rational fear have a useful function. Our remote ancestors came to respect, to fear, the claw and the tooth and the fang of lurking beasts, and such fear had a protective function. Thus is fear a two-edged sword. If allowed to run berserk through the mind of its victim, it is a deadly, crippling, fearsome enemy. If harnessed and made to fit into its proper perspective, fear is a God-given ally and friend.

The day that I left my cardiology friend's office, and for weeks that followed, fear was my enemy—an overpowering, irrational beast of a thing that stole from me my courage, my family, and my will to live. How to use it, how to harness it, how to make it my ally—this was my problem. No easy task, this, but by no means impossible with God!

The days that immediately followed my being tabbed a cardiac patient were, as stated, days of abject depression and paralyzing fear. However stern may be his resolve to face up to the matter, no man can suffer his ambitions, his desires, and his hopes and dreams, especially where two small boys are involved, suddenly to be dashed to earth without feeling that he has, in large measure, died.

For a time I took the medications handed out by the cardiologist, a very respected man in his field, and I heeded insofar as possible his admonition to slow down. Conditions did not permit my taking an extended vacation, however, and even if they had I am certain I would have enjoyed spending the many vacant hours thinking of my solemn plight.

A year or two before this episode, I had become an aficionado of the sport of tennis. At my doctor's bidding I entertained the thought of switching entirely to doubles, and when playing singles I let the tough ones go. But the extra bulge in my pockets (my medications), and the conscious let-up in everything I did were constant reminders that I had joined the ranks of the has-beens, that it was only a matter of rather short time until my *finis* would be complete. When I was with my patients, I constantly was reminded that here was a case of the sick treating the sick. When alone the very walls seemed to close in on me.

But the toughest time of all was when I went home to my two little boys, little guys with whom I had had visions of fishing trips and campouts in faraway places, of baseball and football, and, most of all, of just being there when they needed me in the years to come. And now, chances were I'd never wet a hook with them, never get to see them graduate out of short pants, much less mix it with them in the sports world.

By the end of a week or two of such *welt-schmerz,* I knew I wasn't built for this kind of existence. Something had to give. I'd had quite enough of feeling like Job, who said so many things which I felt like saying myself:

*Wearisome nights are appointed to me. When I lie down, I say, When shall I arise, and the night be gone? and I am full of tossings to and fro unto the dawning of the day. . . . My days are swifter than a weaver's shuttle, and are spent without hope. . . . Mine eye shall no more see good. . . . As the cloud is consumed and vanisheth away: so he that goeth down to the grave shall come up no more. . . . When I say, My bed shall comfort me, my couch shall ease my complaint; Then thou scarest me with dreams, and terrifiest me through visions: So that my soul chooseth strangling, and death rather than my life. I loathe it . . . let me alone; for my days are vanity. (Job 7:1–16)*

It was about here that I chanced (?) across the article on fear about which I spoke in the previous chapter, an article that served as the launching pad for my do-it-yourself assault on fear.

I was well aware of the old adage that a doctor who doctors himself has a nitwit for a doctor and a fool for a patient, and it was never my intent to become my own physician. But I was too curious, compelling so, about the problem that had put me in chains to follow one point of my doctor's advice—which was to "let him do all the thinking" about my problem. I simply had to get the big picture for myself. And that was what, with insatiable curiosity and burning desire, I set out to do.

For the next few months I spent every off afternoon at the medical school, deep in the library stacks, to absorb like a sponge the known and the unknown about coronary heart disease. Quite brashly, at times, though a rank unknown I corresponded with national and international authorities in the various fields related to the problem.

It did not take long to fill many desk drawers with reams of answered and unanswerable questions. I became, in effect, a second-hand authority on the subject, so much so that, years later, after I had evolved and tested my own plan of attack, I wrote a book entitled *Prescription for Life,* which book has received any number of accolades from authoritative sources in the field of physical fitness as it relates to coronary heart desease.

After several weeks of such investigation, eventually I reached a point where I had to decide whether to put some of the theories about vigorous physical exercise to a personal test. The decision meant going against the advice of my physician (not without due deliberation, but after carefully weighing all the evidence at hand). Especially at that time such action would have been termed foolhardy and dangerous by a majority of very capable cardiologists across the land, and I did not make the decision without due consideration of its possible dire consequences: the precipitation of a heart attack, sudden death!

Living under the care of my physician, I could expect, statistically, five to ten years of life before having a heart attack. But what kind of life? That was the question that bugged me. It was, eventually, a bridge of faith—faith in the Lord Jesus Christ—which spanned the gulf of uncertainty that held me in check for many weeks. That bridge of faith led me from a crippled, fearful existence to a full and confident life. About this bridge I have much to say in later chapters. Without it I would never have made the crossing.

# CHAPTER III

# The Facts of the Matter

> To those of you who may be vitalists I would make this
> prophecy: what everyone believed yesterday and you be-
> lieve today, only cranks will believe tomorrow.
> Francis Crick (Nobel prize-winner)

It didn't take a great deal of library probing to find out what
I suspected already—that I was but one of several million people
in this great nation with whom coronary * heart disease deals
harshly, to put it mildly, every year. To be more exact, this disease
is responsible for over 600,000 deaths each year in this country,
and while deaths from blood vessel disease in other organs (in
particular the brain and kidneys) have shown a downward trend
in very recent years, the number from involvement of the coronary
(heart) vessels has continued to rise.

In 1967 there were 106,188 deaths in the 45-to-64 age group
alone. Each time the second hand on the clock sweeps full circle
a victim succumbs. About 30 percent of all deaths in this country
are due to atherosclerotic ** disease of the coronary arteries (those
supplying blood to the heart).

An apparently healthy male, thoroughly evaluated medically by
all the customary methods, runs in a susceptible population about
a one-in-five chance of developing overt coronary disease before
age sixty-five. What's more, some forty percent of initial coronary
attacks bring death within the first four to six weeks, and at least

* The name coronary is derived from the crown-like arrangement of the arteries
supplying the heart muscle itself.

** Atherosclerosis is a process in which atheromata (whey-like lipid deposits) form
in artery linings, with eventual partial or total occlusion of involved vessels.

half of these fatalities occur within the first hour. Of the middle-aged who make a good recovery, 20 percent will be dead in five years, and for victims with complications, the five-year mortality rate is much higher—40 percent, 70 percent, 80 percent or greater, depending on the complication.

Just as appalling as the foregoing facts is the conservative estimate that there are fully as many suspects with coronary heart disease, blithely going about their daily affairs with time bombs in their chests, as there are persons known to be suffering from the disease—on the order of 15 million in each group. No less than one-fourth of the adult population of this country has or may have heart disease, at least 75 percent of which is of the coronary type.

As the saying goes, misery loves company, and there was some small comfort in knowing that my problem was far from being unique. Looking on the bright side, I could in fact rejoice that I had been blessed enough of God to receive a warning in time to meet the problem on my feet instead of in an oxygen tent.

I found out a great many other interesting things about this cruel disease, matters that need not be explored in detail here (some books are listed at the end of this chapter).

First of all, the disease picks on the male a great deal more than it does the female, for reasons as yet incompletely understood (e.g., under age 45, heart disease is five times more common in males than in females). But the female of any age certainly is not spared entirely, and from about age 55 on there is a more similar attack rate in both sexes. No doubt about it, however, under age 55 (and especially under age 45) it pays to be a female insofar as this disease is concerned, at least in the good old U.S.A.

Secondly, coronary heart disease is no respecter of age. In 1963 nearly three fourths of the 707,830 heart deaths occurred in person aged 65 and over. But while primarily a blight of the elderly, coronary disease begins its insidious inroads on the coronary blood vessels decades earlier. It kills the twentyish young man, the thirtyish, the fortyish, just as dead as it does the octogenarian, and, more sadly perhaps, at the peak of a promising career. Witness the recent death of a profootballer at age 28, a well-known football coach in his early forties, and a famous baseball player at 53. Such a list could go on and on.

In populations susceptible to this disease, its earliest indications (fatty streaks in the blood vessel linings) appear in early childhood. Two studies from this country report such lesions being found in all children over three years of age. In the twenties, though deaths from the disease are relatively uncommon, "rusting" of the arteries is well under way, a fact vividly illustrated by a famous study of soldiers killed in the Korean War. In that study of 300 soldiers ranging in age from 19 to 40 years (average age 22), 77 percent showed evidence of coronary disease varying from slight thickening of the lining of the coronary vessels to complete occlusion of one or more main coronary branches. This is indeed damning evidence that coronary blood vessel disease begins its inroads years and decades before it becomes apparent. It is a silent, insidious process; cruel, unrelenting, and unforgiving. As I have stated elsewhere, it is "a hangman who spends years and years building a scaffold and tying a noose only to spring the trapdoor in one split second." *

Finally, coronary heart disease is a costly disease in dollars and cents. Hospital, doctor, and allied incidental services cost its victims billions each year. In 1962 losses caused by such diseases amounted to some 132 million work days, the equivalent of 540,-000 man-years, amounting to losses of $2.5 billion dollars. In the 25–64 age group in that year, more than 1 billion dollars worth of output was lost. The 1962 total loss in output was $24.5 billion. Housewives excluded, the sum of direct costs plus losses of output by members of the labor force due to heart disease is equal to $22.4 billion, or 4 percent of 1962's gross national product.

But dollars and cents statistics cannot begin to measure the real loss—the loss of a breadwinner in the widow's or the orphan's heart; the emotional impact of a vacant seat at the dinner table;

*Prescription For Life, M. F. Graham, David McKay, Inc. (1966), p. 8.

the family tensions springing from a cardiac cripple in the midst of a household, with uncertainty hanging like crepe on the door with each new day; or the length of an hour, nay, of a minute, to a man in his prime, fighting for life in an oxygen tent.

But if coronary heart disease is cruel, and it is, it also is baffling. It has been termed a modern medical jigsaw puzzle, and the more I read about it the more certain I am it deserves this title. One well-known researcher, Dr. M. Friedman of Mount Zion Hospital and Medical Center in San Francisco, has asked of the many causative factors known to play a role in the disease: "Which are the giant redwoods and which are the dwarf banzai trees?" No one knows just yet. A great deal is known about contributing factors. But which comes first? Which is of primary and which of second-ary concern? Which are the main actors and which but the sup-porting cast? Such questions remain unanswered.

A listing of factors must include such a potpourri as: age, sex, race, ethnic background, social class, economic status, family his-tory, body build, personality type; emotional tension, physical inactivity, occupation; caloric intake, total fat intake, cholesterol intake, saturated fat intake, specific fatty acid content of the diet (or a deficiency thereof), carbohydrate and type of carbohydrate intake; blood levels of cholesterol, triglycerides, free fatty acids, beta-lipoproteins, uric acid, sugar, catecholamines; cigarette smok-ing, hypertension, obesity; and, more recently, even the softness of the water supply, along with alcohol and coffee ingestion.

Out of this veritable maze of factors, evidence has evolved from much careful study to spotlight or earmark certain ones as render-ing their possessor "coronary-prone"—i.e., more susceptible to coronary heart disease than the person who does not possess such a factor or factors. Generally accepted as predisposing one to the disease is the presence of one or more of the following factors in his or her makeup:

        1. Hereditary tendency to heart disease, strokes, high blood pressure, diabetes, gout—i.e., the presence of such disease in close relatives, especially under 65 years

of age.
2. A muscular, "athletic" (mesomorphic) type body build.
3. A "driving" personality, as seen in an aggressive, highly competitive individual with a strong sense of urgency as regards time schedules and deadlines.
4. Strong emotional reactions to stressful life situations, especially of a chronic or prolonged nature.
5. Overweight due to excessive fat accumulation (obesity), especially having its beginning after maturity.
6. Diets high in fats (especially animal fats).
7. High blood pressure.
8. Elevated levels of certain biochemical products in the blood, notably certain fatty substances (especially cholesterol) or fats, uric acid, and sugar.
9. Cigarette smoking.
10. Physical inactivity.

In general, the more of the above factors present in a given individual the more susceptible is that individual to coronary heart disease. Moreover, the effect of such factors is additive. For example, a well-known study in Framingham, Mass. revealed an incidence of 1.7 percent cardiovascular disease in males aged 45 to 62 with normal serum cholesterol, with a jump in incidence to 8 percent when serum cholesterol was elevated; but obesity plus hypertension plus elevated serum cholesterol yielded an incidence of 14.3 percent.

Nine years before the writing of this book the author possessed no less than seven, and possibly eight of the foregoing list of predisposing factors: numbers 4, 5, 6, 8, and 10, and, in times of great stress, number 7. Carrying some twenty to twenty-five extra pounds on what should have been a trim and muscular frame, being acutely aware of time schedules and deadlines, going into a frenetic tizzy when under stress, and consuming phenomenal quantities of animal fats, the author's greatest physical effort was walking from hospital or office to automobile, and that no further than the nearest-to-be-found parking space.

Blood cholesterol levels had been a problem for some years, and elevated uric acid in the form of gout came along some seven years ago. Add to these a screw-ball EKG and it is easy to see why the cardiologist took a glum view of my prospects for seeing many more sunrises.

I was, indeed, a sitting duck for a deadly heart attack, and though I have by no means beat the rap, and I have managed to whittle my list of predisposing factors down to near zero; only *near* zero, because now and then I cheat on my diet a bit and my blood cholesterol gets a little out of bounds, though not like it once did; and I do have gout (a hereditary disease), though well-controlled. Nevertheless, gouty individuals do seem to have an increased incidence of cardiovascular disease, controlled or not.

In essence, the story of how I have managed to lick these various items is the story of this book. So what I recount as a physical attack on coronary heart disease has been put to the test; not just by myself, but by countless thousands of researchers and subjects from whom I in turn learned the trick.

Doubtless the reader, and of a certainty the physician-reader, thinks that the simplest thing for me to have done with my broken-down pathological museum of a body was to have dug a hole and crawled in it. And I must admit that there were and are times, even now, especially when adversities pile up, that I heartily agree. But my God by his good pleasure has shown me the path I herein present as the one to take, and I have found it to be, though not easy, a good and glorious one. By his grace I have trodden it now for nine years, and the way is good.

Now, I'm no hero and I've never won any medals for bravery. What's more I'd be a fool to say I wouldn't be anxious in an oxygen tent. Furthermore, EKG (electrocardiograph) machines look like mechanized prophets of doom to me, and Max carts (carts equipped for resuscitation of heartbeat and breathing) might as well be decorated with black crepe paper, as far as I'm concerned. At times, during especially trialsome periods of deep despair, I have thought: "What's the use?" Why not, I have thought, take the advice of Job's wife to "curse God and die?"

All I can say is that during such times God must have been very near, for he always came to the rescue. He forgives me of such despairing thoughts and makes me to know that "underneath are his everlasting arms." In hiding tomorrow from the ken of man, he has taught me to live life one day at a time, and for this I am very glad.

Whether at the next turn of life's road there awaits me, at some unsuspecting moment, a crushing, sledgehammer blow to the chest, signalling a heart attack; whether there is to be sudden, painless cessation of the heartbeat on a tennis court or while jogging down a country lane; or whether there is to be a falling asleep one night, not to awaken here, I do not know. Tomorrow is in God's hands. I can only trust him, as he has taught me to do, that whatever occurs is for my good and his glory. The faithful Christian never forgets that life is fleeting, at best, and that God has promised that "all things will be added unto you" if we "seek first the kingdom of heaven and its rightousness."

Meanwhile, I walk one step at a time in this way which, through study, communication, meditation, and prayer, God has revealed. I have learned to leave tomorrow in his unfailing hands. Would to God that I had learned this lesson decades ago (as a babe in Christ), instead of straying into what seemed greener pastures, following my own inclinations, only to find that such willful peregrinations can lead to only one end: physical and spiritual disease, disaster, and death!

### Some Material of General Interest on Coronary Heart Disease

1. *Your Heart Has Nine Lives.* Blakeslee, Alton, and Stamler, J., M.D. Pocket Books, Inc. New York, N. Y.

2. *Prescription For Life.* Graham, M. F. David McKay Co., Inc. 750 Third Ave. New York, N. Y. 10017.

3. Pamphlets on Coronary Heart Disease for Public Distribution. The American Medical Association. 535 North Dearborn Street. Chicago, Ill. 60610.

4. Pamphlets on Coronary Heart Disease for Public Distribution. The American Heart Association. 44 East 23 Street. New York, N. Y. 10010.

5. *Heart Attack.* Prinzmetal, Myran, M.D. (Available through National Jogging Association, 1832 K Street, N.W., Washington, D. C. 20006.)

6. *Heart Attack: You Don't Have to Die.* Barnard, Christian, M.D. (Available through National Jogging Association—above).

# CHAPTER IV

# Out of the Maze—The Big Three

Which are the giant redwoods and
Which are the dwarf banzai trees?
Meyer Friedman, M.D.

Out of the maze of foregoing factors involved in coronary heart disease it was not difficult to deduce that there are certain ones about which we can do nothing—factors such as one's sex, heredity, predisposition, body build, and personality type or emotional makeup.

Elimination of these factors from consideration leaves, however, a whole gamut of constitutents about which we can do much, and it is obviously with such factors, chiefly environmental and therefore subject to manipulation, that one must be concerned if he is to take the forward, the constructive, look.

Moreover, certain elements in the "coronary profile" of any given individual may require medicinal treatment. Included herein are such diseases as hypertension (high blood pressure), gout, diabetes, and certain types of elevation of the fatty substances in the blood. This is to say that treatment of such facets of the coronary problem as these remain first and foremost in the province of the physician, and secondarily in the domain of the patient. Contrariwise, the remaining factors, though they should be supervised by a physician, remain primarily the responsibility of the patient for execution. The physician, in these realms, can often only advise. He cannot medicate a "correction," as he can in some of the hereditary problems such as gout and diabetes.

Such "primarily patient problems" fall quite naturally into three large categories: the diet-related, the tension-related, and the physical activity-related. These I have termed the *Big Three*. A fourth and equally important problem, cigarette smoking, is not considered here in depth because it did not apply in my own case.

As pointed out by any number of well known investigators, these factors have stemmed from a way of life; in this instance, the American way, characterized by a diet rich in total fat, and in particular cholesterol and "hard" animal fat; by a competitive, time-conscious, tension-oriented social structure; and by physical inactivity. We are a rich nation, an affluent people, and the hallmarks of our wealth are fat food; fat bank accounts that stem from an economy based on private wealth and enterprise, a system which thrives on competition, and which by its very nature engenders tension; and a sweatless, white-collar environment of wheels, push buttons, and levers which do the multitudinous tasks that man once did by the sweat of his brow.

Such is our heritage, the product of a rich land, an industrious, competitive people, and the march of science. It has been a long and arduous way from the farm to the forum, from the forest to the factory, from blue denim overalls to nattily-pressed business suits; and we have somehow concluded, as a people, that we are entitled to enjoy our air-conditioned environments and our marbled steaks. After all, we have worked for them, fought for them. We have paid the price, and now is the time to lie back and, with gadgets and machinery to do our physical work, sate the gut and take stock of our dollar-marked success.

But we have wallowed so hoggishly in our new-found "freedoms" that not until recently have our men of medicine brought to light the backwash of diseased blood vessels and hearts that the "good life" has produced. We have been so intent on our gadgeteering, our dollar-making, and the rich foods and fast wheels that dollars can buy that we have failed to see the Frankenstein that we have created, the "white plague" which threatens our most vital possession, our health, both as individuals and as a nation.

The "Big Three" concept (or Big Four, including cigarette

smoking), that diet, tension, and physical inactivity represent the triad of factors best lending themselves to personal manipulation in the problem of cardiovascular disease, is borne out by the recommendations of numerous authorities, both individual and organizational, in attacking the problem. I cite some of them here.

It is noteworthy that, hereditary and medicinally-oriented problems (such as high blood pressure, gout, and diabetes) aside, any of the following recommendations may be catergorized under one of the Big Three—dietary measures, anti-tension measures, and measures designed to promote physical activity. Even the highly hazardous habit of cigarette smoking may be a manifestation of tension, if not of a certain personality-type.

American Heart Association dietary recommendations (1965):[1]

1. Eat less animal (saturated) fat.
2. Increase intake of vegetable oils and other polyunsaturated fats, substituting them for saturated * fats wherever possible.
3. Eat less food rich in cholesterol (see p. 37).
4. If overweight, reduce caloric intake to achieve and maintain desirable weight.
5. Apply these dietary recommendations early in life.
6. Maintain principles of good nutrition. Professional advice may be necessary.
7. Adhere consistently to the above dietary recommendations so that a decrease in the concentration of fatty substances in the blood may be both achieved and maintained.
8. Make sound food habits a "family affair."

Dr. Jeremiah Stamler, reknowned heart specialist of Chicago,

---

[1] See bibliography, *Periodicals,* number 5. Though minor revisions were made in 1968, the basic tenets as stated here remain the same.

* Saturated, or so-called "hard" fats, are those which are solid at room temperature (ex.: lard, butter, the "marble" in beef and pork), as opposed to unsaturated (especially polyunsaturated) fats, which are liquid at room temperature (ex.: most vegetable oils). A list of the type of foods rich and poor in cholesterol are listed at the end of the chapter, along with books and pamphlets on the subject.

Illinois, in an address to the Second National Conference on Cardiovascular Disease in November, 1964,[2] listed these cautions:

1. Maintain a diet low in fats, especially saturated fats, with weight reduction where necessary.
2. Stop heavy cigarette smoking.
3. Maintain a regimen providing continuous muscle-toning exercise.
4. Medically manage high blood pressure.

Dr. Paul Dudley White, dean of American cardiologists cautions: [3]

1. Lose excess weight.
2. Limit fats not to exceed 30 percent of calories, of which ¾ are unsaturated.
3. Adopt a program of regular exercise to continue throughout life (to quote): "Studies are proving more and more that the person who burns up his calories by hard physical work or exercise does not so soon develop atherosclerosis."
4. Avoid cigarettes.
5. Avoid excessive stress insofar as possible.

The American Heart Association in its 1964 annual report, advises: [4]

1. Reduce if overweight.
2. Decrease saturated fats in the diet.
3. Stop smoking cigarettes.
4. Control high blood pressure.
5. Exercise regularly.
6. Shun needless tensions.

Dr. E. Grey Dimond, formerly of the famous Scripps Clinic in La Jolla, California, now professor of medicine at the University of Missouri, in noting that the peak age for angina (heart pain) in this country is 42 years (as compared to 52 in other countries), cites

[2] See bibliography, *Periodicals,* number 16, Jan. 15, 1965.
[3] See bibliography, *Periodicals,* number 8.
[4] See bibliography, *Periodicals,* number 15, Mar. 8, 1965.

four possible reasons, which he obviously would reverse to attack the problem: [5]

1. The stress and strain of the American way of life.
2. The competitive society.
3. The lack of exercise.
4. The American diet.

"The only other nation," says Dr. Dimond, "which offers a similar pattern of high, aggressive, competitive, frenetic, anxious living, is West Germany. And in that country more and more men are suffering from more and more coronary disease at an earlier age. Soon, they will get down to our level."

Dr. Irving Page, Director of Research at the Cleveland Clinic Foundation, said in an interview: "I think the answer lies in establishing a way of life in which diet and other factors will receive proper emphasis. . . . Live as though you were going to live forever. . . . Maintain your weight somewhere near the level of your youth; find a way of life to keep it there, but not from periodic dieting; a simple way is to reduce fat calories from the usual 45 to 25 percent. . . . Keep your body fit with regular exercise. . . . Adopt a philosophy of moderation in all things." [6]

Dr. W. Raab, Professor of Experimental Medicine at the University of Vermont, doubtless would favour reversal or abolition of the "three elements of prosperous, civilized living . . . known to create a potentially fatal" metabolism in the heart: "(1) emotional stresses, (2) lack of physical exercise . . . (3) nicotine." [7] At the First International Conference on Preventive Cardiology at the University of Vermont, Dr. Raab pointed out that "these long disregarded facts were emphatically reconfirmed by a host of experimental and clinical data from several countries." Dr. Raab's extensive volume, *Prevention of Ischemic Heart Disease,* catalogues such data beautifully and convincingly.

Dr. White (cited above), at a recent American College of Cardi-

---

[5] See bibliography, *Periodicals,* number 19.

[6] See bibliography, *Periodicals,* number 18, Dec. 1, '57.

[7] See bibliography, *Periodicals,* number 15, Dec. 23, '64.

ology meeting, [8] pointed out that increasing numbers of studies confirm that "an active muscular metabolism due to physical exercise suited to the individual over the years delays or even prevents any important clinical manifestations of atherosclerosis of essential arteries." Dr. Stamler (also cited above) contends that countless deaths from premature heart disease might be averted by the simple application of present knowledge.

Such statements and recommendations stem from decades of intensive studies that fill entire shelves and sections of medical libraries. The amount of research and thought and endeavor behind each recommendation truly is astounding and far too voluminous more than to allude to here. The first thing I would have the reader note about these recommendations is their positive, do-something attitude. The second thing is that regular exercise is the natural vanguard of action which reinforces all other measures and renders them far easier to achieve. Physical activity is, in fact, the common denominator of attack on the Big Three.

As will become obvious, physical activity is the logical springboard of action to launch one's personal physical campaign against coronary heart disease. It is the key to doing battle against those factors which fall largely within the realm and responsibility of the individual's own will and power, as opposed to those of the physician; and it will open many vital doors which otherwise would slam shut with a foreboding finality.

## About Cholesterol

Cholesterol is a fatty substance, really a complex alcohol (a sterol), normally present in animal tissue. Its presence in the blood of coronary-prone persons in abnormally large amounts is associated with an increased incidence of heart attacks.

Diets aimed at reducing susceptibility to a heart attack in such persons must contain little or no egg yolk, butterfat (including cream, whole milk, and cheese), animal fat (such as visible fat of

[8] See bibliography, *Periodicals,* number 15, Dec. 23, '64.

meat, lard, pork fat, bacon fat, chicken fat, suet), and organ meats (variety meats, such as brains, liver, giblets), all of which are high in cholesterol. Since animal fats contain some cholesterol, the fat intake must also be restricted. All possible meat fat should be removed, and fat in meat drippings and in broth and soup stock should be avoided. Other foods commonly containing fat include many bakery products (cakes, pies, cookies, doughnuts, pastry); many packaged mixes for cakes, pancakes, waffles, puddings; commercial mayonnaise; some canned soups. All fats of vegetable origin (such as margarines, vegetable oils like cottonseed, soybean, corn, peanut, and olive) may be used in limited amounts.

### Recommended Reading Material

1. *The Low Fat, Low Cholesterol Diet,* by Dobbin, E. Virginia, Gefman, Helen F., et al. Doubleday & Co. Copyright 1951 by Virginia E. Dobbin.

2. *Dietary Control of Cholesterol.* Fleischmann's Margarines. 625 Madison Ave. New York, N. Y. 10022.

3. Pamphlets on Dieting Against Heart Disease. The American Medical Association. 535 North Dearborn Street. Chicago, Ill. 60610.

4. Booklet # EM 455, *The Way to a Man's Heart,* and #455A, *Recipes For Fat-Controlled, Low Cholesterol Meals.* The American Heart Association. 44 East 23 Street. New York, N. Y. 10010.

5. *Prescription For Life.* by M. F. Graham, M.D. David McKay Company, Inc., 1966. 750 Third Avenue. New York, N. Y. 10017.

# CHAPTER V

# Physical Exercise—The Common Denominator

Health, like happiness, is to be found,
If at all,
By the wayside,
And the more you pursue it,
The more it flees from you.
                        Sir Robert Hutchison

Careful consideration of the Big Three factors—diet, tension, and physical activity—made it quite obvious to me that a proper program of physical fitness well could serve as a common denominator for attacking this lethal triad, inasmuch as physical exercise has a dieting and an anti-tensive effect locked in. Such is not the case for either dieting or passive anti-tension measures, in themselves.

In a nutshell, adequate physical exercise consumes fats in the flame of action, and tension melts beneath its influence like butter on a hot plate. A closer look at the mechanisms involved are in order at this stage.

## Role of Exercise in Dieting

There are two major aspects to dieting: the quantitative and the qualitative. The first of these, the quantitative, relates to caloric balance, and thus the control of body weight; the second of these, the qualitative, refers to the proportions in which the major kinds of foodstuffs—protein, carbohydrate, and fat—are consumed, as well as to form (e.g., saturated or unsaturated fats) of each.

## 1. The Quantitative Aspect of Dieting

When the number of calories consumed exceeds the number expended over a significant period of time, they are stored in the body as fat, and weight is gained. Contrariwise, when the calories expended exceed the number consumed in a like period, fat stores are used up and weight is lost. These simplified truths form the foundation for the role of exercise in maintaining desirable, or ideal, weight.

A pound of fat stores some 4000 calories. Thus, theoretically, the loss of a pound of fat requires the utilization by the body of about 4000 calories in excess of the number consumed during the perod in which that pound is lost. Riding a bicycle some 15 m.p.h. (a good clip) requires the expenditure of some 12 calories per minute. Thus, riding a bicycle at this rate for on hour burns up some 720 calories. Accordingly, five hours of bike riding at a fast clip rids the body of nearly one pound of fat, if no calories are consumed and if this is the only consideration.

However, other factors come into play, such as the increased utilization of sugar, some protein loss, sweating, and so on, and such figures are therefore but rough approximations. The basic concept, however, is correct. Exercise speeds up the utilization of body stores of fat, and an overweight individual who includes exercise in his reducing regimen can greatly facilitate the loss of excess weight. Very simply, exercise requires fuel, and the more vigorous and/or the longer its duration, the more fuel is required. And stored body fat is one major source of fuel.

Likewise, after one has attained desirable body weight, the incorporation of regular exercise programs into one's way of life enables that person to maintain an equilibrium between calories consumed and calories expended with remarkable ease and steadfastness, and with a great deal more satisfaction.

As a matter of fact, the use of improper dieting alone as a means of losing weight, or of maintaining desirable weight, can be fraught with considerable danger. Crash diets, for example, cause weight loss primarily at the expense of body protein—muscle mass—

rather than fat. Still others can lead to serious vitamin deficiencies if approached haphazardly. Once desirable weight is attained via the exercise route, one can often satiate his appetite to his heart's content by striking a balance between caloric intake and caloric output.

On the other hand, the use of exercise alone as a means of weight reduction is to be decried. Until desirable body weight is attained, at least, the combination of sensible dieting and sensible exercise yields by the far the best results by the easiest and the most physiologic of routes.

## 2. The Qualitative Aspect of Dieting

The "all-American" diet derives some 40 percent, and often more of its calories from fat, most of which is of the saturated or "hard" variety. Moreover, included in this lard mill is enough cholesterol to insure the progressive rusting of millions upon millions of arteries in our population for decades to come. The incrimination of such diets in the development of the cheese-like rust (atheroma) in arterial linings is well documented in the medical literature. A mere listing of all source material would require more pages than are in this entire book. For all too high a percentage of Americans such a diet is pure poison. Hence the recommendation from sources already cited to lower the fat consumption to no more than 30 percent of one's total caloric intake, and to substitute unsaturated (liquid at room temperature) fats for saturated (hard at room temperature) fats whenever possible. Numerous studies in which such dietary measures have been instituted have yielded convincing evidence that the incidence of coronary heart disease can be significantly lowered in the dieting group.

The question here on the carpet is: can physical exercise in any measure bring about, or facilitate, the effect of such diets? Can exercise similarly lower blood cholesterol and serum triglyceride * levels, as such diets are capable of doing? The answer to this question is not at all clear. Some studies seem to indicate that

---

* Triglycerides are neutral fats which constitute such fat as that in beef, pork, and dairy products. They are composed of fatty acids combined with glycerol.

exercise can and does result in lower levels of blood lipids (fatty substances), especially if the initial levels are high. Other studies are not so conclusive.

There is some indication that a vigorous exerciser may eat pretty well what he wants, as long as he maintains desirable weight by getting rid of the calories on the track or the bicycle or in the swim. The careful investigator of the literature cannot yet draw such firm conclusions, although lowering of triglycerides by exercise is more predictable than the lowering of cholesterol by similar means. However, there is no doubt that if exercise does exert an effect on the qualitative aspect of dieting, it is a salutory one. At best, probably, the lowering of elevated blood lipids by exercise *per se* is a highly individual phenomenon. It depends on the type, degree, and cause of lipid elevation and the total individual in whom it occurs.

But the assumption that fat and/or cholesterol are the only considerations in the American diet may be only partially true. There is some evidence, though not widely accepted, that the carbohydrate content of the diet may be equally important, especially in certain individuals. In particular, the use of large quantities of refined and simple carbohydrates—such as table sugar, jams and jellies, pastries and the like—as opposed to the more complex carbohydrates such as bread and cereals, has taken on special significance in many eye-opening studies. Such sugars may be responsible for the elevation of lipids in certain individuals, and thus may be the real culprits, rather than fatty foods, behind the lipid aberration.

There is little doubt that physical exercise plays an insulinogenic role—it "burns" sugar. As a tool in the treatment of diabetes, exercise long has been held in high esteem. Why? Simply because of this sugar-utilizing effect.

So when one considers the overall qualitative dietary picture, it is difficult to believe that a good exercise program can do less than facilitate whatever dietary measures are deemed necessary in a given individual. The debate, it would seem, is not whether or not such a service is performed, but rather to what extent in a given subject.

## Role of Exercise in Combating Tension

Tension is the subjective and objective product of stress. Subjective evidence includes such feelings as apprehension, frustration, uncertainty, doubt, fear. Objective evidence consists of increased pulse rates, higher blood pressure, and increased muscle tension, among a number of other physiologic criteria. Tension, then, may be viewed as the sum total of the inner reaction of the individual to a threat to his secure status quo, whether the threat be internal or external. To be sure, tension is a much more involved phenomenon than this, but for our purposes such a concept will suffice.

Stress may take many forms. It may be acute, as when one suddenly awakens and finds his bedroom in flames. Or it may be chronic, as when one harbors, over the years, smouldering resentments against the boss, a wife, or a competitor.

As an analogy, if tension is represented by a rubber band on stretch, stress is the force that applies the stretch. Short-term stretching will not prohibit the return of the band to its former length and profile on release. No so with long-term tension, the effect of which is to prevent the return of the band, on release, to its former length and elasticity. Similarly, in the biologic analogy, short-term tension, finding quick release, serves a useful and protective function. But chronic tension distorts, resets, re-regulates such body functions as pulse rates and blood pressure and lipid and sugar levels. They remain chronically elevated in many individuals, for release that does not come. And thus does chronic tension defeat the very purpose for which tension was originally designed—to protect the organism. Thus does defender turn destroyer.

Study the figure on the following page. It traces the effect of stress (danger) on the organism, to show how fear, upon being recognized, triggers off a chain reaction mediated through the endocrine glands (glands which secrete hormones directly into the

# THE FIGHT OR FLIGHT (ADRENERGIC) RESPONSE[1]

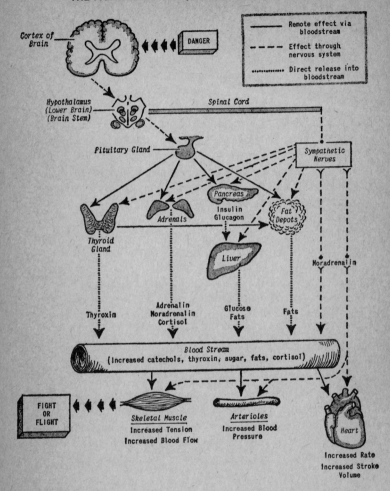

bloodstream) and the autonomic nervous system *. Note that in response to the threat, this "neuro-hormonal" axis brings about a release of fuel (fat and sugar) into the blood stream along with a variety of hormones whose function is to make that fuel available and to metabolize (burn) it in order that the body may meet the threat.

The heightened pulse rate and blood pressure, the increased muscle tension, the increased levels of hormones and fats and sugars in the blood, all are preparatory to enabling the organism either to fight or flee from the threat—a protective mechanism. In a society where fight or flight is often verboten, taboo, social suicide, such bodily reactions are bottled up inside over lengthy periods, with the result that blood lipids remain elevated, as do blood pressures and pulse rates, all factors that predispose one to a heart attack. The figure on the next page illustrates this vicious cycle of modern civilization, a rat race in which man is on stretch for year after year, without surcease, without relief, without release.

* The autonomic nervous system is that autonomous division of the nervous system which autonomously and automatically regulates reactions (such as pulse and blood pressure), involuntary bodily processes over which we have no voluntary control (i.e. involuntary). The very term *autonomic* implies self-regulating.

---

*Diagram:* This response is a complex, primitive one in which the body is physiologically prepared to do battle with, or to flee, an imminent danger. Under the influence of the brain, the endocrine glands release the necessary materials into the blood stream, with a resultant increase in blood pressure, heart rate, muscle tension, and flow of blood to the skeletal muscles in particular. The normal means of releasing the stored-up tension resulting from this "adrenergic" response is through the skeletal muscles—i.e., through exercise. When such release is not available to the body, heart and blood-vessel disease is aggravated (see text). Modern-day tensions of living produce the same overall effect as external dangers, but modern civilization denies man the fight-or-flight release, except through exercise.

[1] Diagrams from *Prescription For Life,* M. F. Graham, New York: David McKay Co., Inc., 1966. Used by permission.

## THE TENSION CYCLE IN MODERN CIVILIZATION

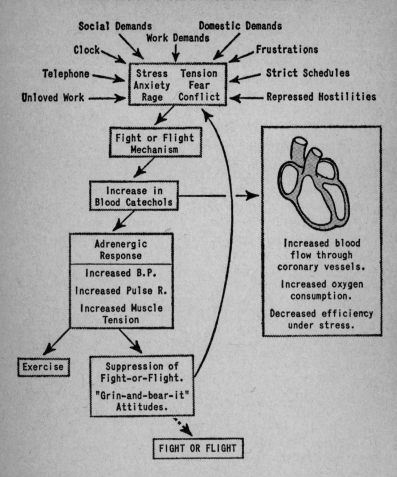

*Diagram:* Physiologically, modern man responds to the tensions of modern living in much the same manner that he does to danger. The same fight-or-flight mechanism is set in motion repeatedly, with a damaging chronically recurrent elevation in blood catechols (adrenalin and noradrenalin) leading to a chronically recurring adrenergic response (Fig.). But in modern society fight

The natural and acceptable outlet for fight or flight is physical exercise, as vigorous as time and conditions permit. In the aftermath of muscular action pulse rates and blood pressures fall, blood lipid levels come down, and tension melts away. Why? Because, physiologically speaking, leisure-time physical activity is the precise equivalent of fight or flight. Thus may one on a tennis court or a track release the pentup storehouses of tension and come away just as though he had done physical combat with or had run from the stress of the day. He "unstretches" himself. He relaxes. He releases. He gives outlet to the physiologic and mental processes stored up within him and comes away a different man. In the aftermath of vigorous physical pursuit, resting pulse rates are slower, blood pressures lower, muscles pleasantly "unlaxed," the mind unwound. The potentially noxious, though physiologic, materials that have responded to the call of muscle and sinew—the lipids, the sugars, the catechols,* the other hormones—have been utilized. Their tension-producing effect has been soundly punctured.

### Effects of Exercise on the Heart and Peripheral Blood Supply

The heart, though a four-chambered organ, is in reality two separate pumps, consisting of two chambers each, arranged in series. One pump, the right side of the heart, consists of a chamber (the right atrium) for receiving unoxygenated (venous) blood from all parts of the body, and a pumping chamber (the right ventricle), whose function it is to pump blood to the lungs for oxygenation.

* Hormones, chiefly adrenalin and noradrenalin, manufactured by the inner portion, or medulla, of the adrenal glands.

---

or flight, the natural skeletal muscle outlet for these tensions is blocked by suppressions, repressions, and "grin-and-bear-it" attitudes. The result is the vicious cycle of still more stress, anxiety, et al. Exercise is the perfect substitute for fight or flight, a readily available and natural means of breaking the cycle.

## DIAGRAM OF HEART

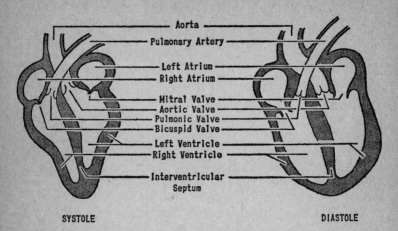

Aorta
Pulmonary Artery
Left Atrium
Right Atrium
Mitral Valve
Aortic Valve
Pulmonic Valve
Bicuspid Valve
Left Ventricle
Right Ventricle
Interventricular
Septum

SYSTOLE                                                    DIASTOLE

*Diagram:* Systole is the pumping, or ejection, phase of the heartbeat. Diastole is the filling, or resting, phase. During filling, the ventricles expand as blood flows into them from the atria, or auricles. The right auricle receives oxygen-poor blood from all parts of the body, while the left auricle receives freshly oxygenated blood from the lungs. Note that during diastole, therefore, the valves between atria and ventricles are open and the valves in the main blood vessels leaving the heart (the pulmonary artery and aorta) are closed. During systole, when the heart is performing its work, the ventricles contract as the valves connecting them with the auricles close and the valves in the major blood vessels open. Thus oxygen-poor blood is forced from the right ventricle through the pulmonary artery to the lungs for oxygenation, and the freshly oxygenated blood in the left ventricle is distributed to all parts of the body through the great aorta.

The right heart is a low pressure system under normal circumstances. The left side of the heart consists of the left atrium, which receives oxygenated blood from the lungs, and the left ventricle, the real work horse of the heart, whose function it is to pump oxygenated blood to all parts of the body. The left side of the heart, the ventricle in particular, is a high-pressure system.

The function of this highly specialized muscular organ about the size of one's fist is to pump blood—day in and day out, hour after hour, minute after minute, second after second. The resting heart, beating (for example) 72 times per minute, beats over 100,000 times per day. With each beat it ejects up to three ounces of blood from each ventricle. The left ventricle, during contraction, works against an average mean pressure of 85 mm. of mercury, which is equivalent to a vertical water column (water pressure) of about 46 inches, and propels the blood in the aorta at a mean velocity of some 16 inches per second. Thus the left ventricle, beating at a rate of 60 times per minute, each minute may move nearly 1½ gallons of blood an approximate distance of 1½ feet, pumping a staggering total of some 2000 gallons of blood per day. Though multiplied many times by frictional resistance, this task, uncomplicated, would be roughly equivalent to lifting some 12 tons through a distance of one foot, a truly prodigious feat.

Obviously, such a veritably indefatigable type of muscle, unable to rest in the same manner in which skeletal muscle rests, requires an especially rich blood supply. The two coronary vessels, arising from the aorta itself at the base of the heart, are the chief source of this supply. Every fiber of heart muscle is bathed in blood supplied by the coronary vessels, each individual fiber possibly having its own capillary vessel. The coronary vessels, but a fraction of an inch in diameter at their origin, divide and subdivide into eventual sinusoidal (spongy) spaces which surround the heart fibers. These spaces communicate with each other and, through special tiny vessels, with the interior of the heart chambers themselves. So vascular is the heart that implantation of a bleeding artery into its substance (as is done in one operation for coronary heart disease) does not cause the blood to accumulate in a pool as it would in other types of tissue. This is possible only because blood is so rapidly picked up and circulated through the heart's vast circulatory system. In short, the heart is naturally endowed with the necessary blood supply for performing fantastic amounts of work.

## DIAGRAM OF ARTERIES IN CROSS-SECTION
## SHOWING THE PROCESS OF ATHEROMATOSIS
(ATHEROSCLEROSIS) ("HARDENING" OF THE ARTERIES)

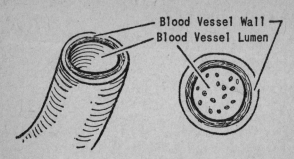

Blood Vessel Wall
Blood Vessel Lumen

NORMAL ARTERY

Fatty Streaks in Lining

MINIMAL ATHEROSCLEROSIS

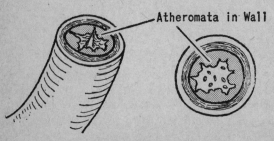

Atheromata in Wall

MARKED ATHEROSCLEROSIS

The heart at work and during exercise is capable of tripling its resting rate, increasing its volume output 500 or even 600 percent, and increasing its total work by more than 1000 percent. The amount of oxygen inhaled by an individual also is a good measure of the working capacity of that person's heart. Air intake may jump from 6 to 8 liters per minute (one liter equals approximately one quart) in a normal man at rest to as much as 100 liters during vigorous muscular activity, with an increase in oxygen transfer across the alveoli (air sacs) of the lungs from 0.3 to 5 liters. The heart increases its work ability by increasing its rate as well as its stroke volume (amount of blood ejected per stroke). In so doing, its oxygen requirement may be increased twelve times or so. The extraction of oxygen from arterial blood entering its muscle becomes much more efficient, by a magnitude that may reach 350 percent.

It requires no great stretch of the imagination to see what narrowing or constriction of the coronary arteries by the disease proc-

---

*Diagram:* The real villain in blood-vessel disease is the process known as atheromatosis, or atheroma formation. Atheromas are cheesy deposits (plaques) in vessel walls which protrude into and encroach on vessel lumens so that areas supplied by vessels thus involved may have their blood supply compromised and, eventually, cut off completely, either by the plaques themselves or by clots which readily form on the plaques, or by hemorrhage into the diseased vessel wall. In the early stages of formation atheromata are little more than fatty streaks which merely corrugate the normally smooth lining of the blood vessels, but over the years they may enlarge enormously, until little or no room remains for the flow of blood. When the vessels thus involved are the coronary arteries, heart disease results.

Atheromas are formed primarily of fats of the type normally present in the blood-stream. Although chiefly cholesterol, fats of the saturated (fatty acid) type also are found in large quantity in the plaques. Eventually, however, scar tissue may replace the fatty materials, and finally calcification may occur, rendering the plaques hard and bony (sclerosis or "hardening").

Many factors contribute to this relentless process (see text), but exercise is a potent factor in preventing, arresting, or possibly even reversing (in the early phase of fatty infiltration) its lethal course.

ess called atherosclerosis (see diagram on page 50) will do to as active a muscle as that of the heart. To deprive this remarkable organ of maximum function over long periods of time is an invitation to disaster. It is much akin to putting an arm in a sling; the muscles wither and atrophy, and soon the arm is capable of performing but a fracton of the work of which it originally was capable. Then, when suddenly called upon for strenuous exertion, it is unable to rise to the occasion. Commonly, in the case of the untrained heart, this results in a heart attack, as grimly exemplified by an October, 1965, newspaper article that cited the following boxscore for big game hunters in a section of Colorado: three shot to death, one crushed under a jeep, and seven dead of heart attacks!

In youth, barring structural defect or involvement by childhood disease, the heart is a remarkably strong organ, capable of prodigious effort. It is only through misuse and disuse that it becomes in so many middle-aged males a crippled, faulty piece of machinery that must be nursed and coddled along like an invalid throughout the remainder of its foreshortened, danger-fraught years.

The effect of regular and proper exercise on the heart seems, basically, to be threefold: (1) to increase the collateral blood supply to heart muscle in certain instances where it is compromised; (2) to increase the efficiency of the heart as a machine (pump); (3) to render the heart less vulnerable to such potentially toxic substances as huge quantities of catecholamines (adrenalin and noradrenalin).

Collateral blood supply refers to new or supplemental channels formed to supply an area of muscle whose original blood supply partially has been cut off. There is good experimental evidence that in some cases regular, properly programed exercise stimulates the formation of such collateral. This is the most likely explanation of the generally accepted thesis that regular exercisers have a higher survival rate from heart attacks than do non-exercisers, although some reports cast doubt on this tenet. It may also explain how some patients who have had heart attacks can, with assiduous and faithful attention to good exercise programs, develop a level of cardiac function which surpasses that which they had prior to their attacks.

Increased efficiency of the heart refers to its ability to perform the same amount of work with less effort. The effect of regular exercise, in this regard, is to enable the heart to pump more blood per stroke, both at rest and during exercise. Thus the trained heart moves the same amount of blood with less effort (fewer strokes) than the untrained heart. This effect is reflected in the slower resting (or exercising) pulse rates found in athletes and in persons who maintain good exercise programs. Involved at the cellular level is greater oxygen economy, with more complete extraction and utilization of oxygen from arterial blood.

Adrenalin and noradrenalin (catecholamines which are hormones secreted by the adrenal medulla, the inner portion of the adrenal gland) are physiologic "pepper-uppers" of the heart. They bring about a simultaneous rise in pulse rate, blood pressure, muscle tension, and a release of fuels (sugars and fats) into the bloodstream preparatory to fight or flight. Under proper circumstances, and in proper quantity, the function of these substances is physiologic. But in excessive quantities, under conditions not designed for their immediate and full and proper utilization, these materials can be deadly to heart muscle or to the heart itself.

Numerous studies have supported the role of these substances in necrosis (death) of tiny areas of heart muscle when circulating in large amounts. Not only can they cause death of heart muscle under such circumstances, but they also are capable of triggering off deadly arrhythmias of the heart. Sudden exertion by poorly conditioned persons, or sudden anger or fright, are capable of causing such sudden death. Witness the deer hunters who die each year from dragging their kill down mountain trails, or the victims of tornadoes who die not from the storms, but from heart attacks triggered by fright.

John Hunter, a famous physiologist and surgeon, was victim of angina (heart pain), and rightfully contended that he was at the mercy of any scalawag who dared to antagonize him. Sure enough, immediately upon the heels of a violent disagreement with some of his colleagues, John Hunter was seized with severe chest pain and died of a heart attack shortly thereafter.

The trained heart is better able to cope with what might otherwise prove to be deadly quantities of the catecholamines, presumably because vigorous exercise accustoms the organ to metabolism of large helpings of these two-edged swords.

Not all of the training effect of exercise revolves around the heart, of course. Skeletal muscle becomes more vascular, likewise, and better able to utilize the oxygen provided it. The pumping action of skeletal muscle on veins returning blood to the heart is enhanced. The oxygen-carrying capacity of the blood itself is increased (via an increase in red blood cell numbers) along with the ability of the various tissues to extract it from the blood at the cellular level. And the volume of blood increases. Neither room nor intent here allows a full explanation of all the marvellous and intricate mechanisms involved. In my book, *Prescription for Life*, I have explored in much greater detail the entire array of such mechanisms, and the reader is referred to that volume and to its bibliography if interested in such detail.*

Suffice it to say that if the untrained body is a thing of beauty, as indeed it is, then the trained body is a thing of ultimate beauty, for it is performing in the superlative fashion for which its physical machinery was intended. A race horse in the stall may be a beautiful animal, but it is when he is roaring down the stretch, mane flying and sweat glistening on his hide, that he is a picture of his true self, achieving that for which he was born. The machinery of the body may eventually wear out, as indeed it will, but it should never be allowed to rust out, artery by vital artery. A sensible, regularly pursued exercise program is the best guarantee against such an event yet provided by our Creator. It is my firm conviction that of those Christians to whom he has given sound bodies God expects no less than the best of care for these earthly temples.

* Much of the data in this chapter is taken verbatim from *Prescription For Life,* with permission of the publisher, David McKay, Inc., New York, N. Y.

Having been assured by such considerations as the foregoing, then, that physical exercise is the hub of the wheel around which the other spokes for attacking the heart disease problem revolve, I was faced with the question of the how and the how much of exercise.

The how was not too tough a question to answer. All indications were that the best kind of exercise to do the job I wanted it to do would have to be of a rhythmic type involving the leg muscles. The physical pursuit that best lent itself to this requirement was jogging, or running, although swimming or cycling (if done vigorously enough), or even walking (especially in the early phases of conditioning) were all very good. As stated elsewhere, I settled on jogging, for a number of reasons. I could do it alone, at any time of day or night, and the equipment required was minimal. Moreover, I could set my own pace and increase it as leisurely as my heart desired. Also, no weather short of a driving rain would necessarily keep me from performing my duly appointed rounds out-of-doors, and for one who deplores running indoors (in-place), this was important.

Accordingly, I laid out a one-mile course around a bevy of neighborhood blocks and began. The method I used I have termed the two-miles-or-bust method, which, very simply, consisted of traversing the one mile course two times every night of the week, at first as a walk; than as a combination walk and jog (walk fifty paces, then run fifty); then eventually as a jog all the way. The time required for going from all walk to all jog, then all run, was something on the order of three months, as I recall. The guide lines I used in adjusting my rate of conditioning were, primarily: (1) the rate of pulse recovery (the time required for my pulse to return to resting levels after the exercise); (2) the presence or absence of "hangover fatigue" (fatigue or too-rapid pulse rates existing into the night or the following day). If my pulse rate still was above resting levels two hours following exercise, or if I was dogged by fatigue of a type that exceeded a pleasant, relaxed feeling for hours afterward, I knew I was trying to move along too fast, and so I slowed down.

Eventually, I was able to easily traverse the two-mile course in 15 or 16 minutes, whereupon I began to run even greater distances, up to five miles on occasion. But I took the utmost care to adjust my progress according to certain rules which have been more explicitly presented in *Prescription For Life.*

Some two years after the appearance of my book, however, Dr. Ken Cooper's *Aerobics* was released, and the problem of how and how much was solved with laboratory precision. Surprisingly, I fit into the "good" category for men of my age, but the truly amazing thing was that I had achieved this level of fitness using much the same technique recommended by Dr. Cooper; and I had done it before I ever knew of this man or read his excellent book (which, incidentally, I heartily recommend to all who anticipate taking up or continuing in a fitness program). For the fitness enthusiast, Dr. Cooper has made it obsolete to grope one's way along the jogging trail. Upon reading his book in the wake of my own experience, I stood amazed at the guidance given me by an Unseen Hand. It was almost as though I had had a copy of *Aerobics* in hand long before it was published! Truly, the Lord my God was with me whithersoever I went.


The attack upon dietary habits that have long stood, life routines that engender tension, and physical inactivity, involves self discipline, singleness of purpose, and pure hard work. It is not a royal road to glory. But it pays handsome dividends.

Certainly its requirements are such that in my own strength I could not have achieved the end-point I was able to reach. For this strength I give God all the credit and the glory. More than once along the way I was tempted to sit back in an easy chair, turn on the TV, and let science do it, leave it to the internist and the surgeon. The rapid advances in heart surgery, in particular, enticingly tempted me to take the easy way out. *Why fight it,* I thought more than once. *Why not leave it to medicine?*

Here let me interject that the surgeons have done a tremendous job in attacking coronary heart disease. I doff my hat to their courage and their vision and their capability. But they do not have the ultimate answer. Not yet.

Heart transplantation, for example, temporarily has been suspended as an experimental procedure, as it will likely remain until the problem of tissue rejection is licked. When will that be? Since Dr. Christian Barnard's first historic transplant in December of 1967, nearly 200 such procedures have been done, with but a handful (about 28) of survivors. The rejection phenomenon and the donor problems, with all the legalistic and moral implications, remain to be solved.

But even were the solution to these problems already at hand, there would be enough surgical teams available to service but an infinitesimal portion of the long line of candidates. A few hundred might be salvaged, while thousands died-a-waiting. The problems facing successful heart transplantation are by no means insoluble, but they are formidable, and no immediate solution is in sight.

Mechanical hearts, or mechanical assist devices, are a likely alternate, or intermediate means of bridging the gap until the heart transplant problem is lifted from the realm of experimentation into that of acceptable procedure. But here again, where are the hands to do the job on more than a miniscule portion of the candidates, even were all the problems related to mechanical devices already solved (which they are not)? Doctor shortage in this area is a very real problem, one which may well get worse before it gets better. And heart surgeons certainly are not trained in a day.

Surgical attack on the coronary problem is not a new vista at all. It dates back some two or three decades, at least. There are a dozen or more surgical procedures in use today for improving blood supply to the heart, all of which have met with varying degrees of success, none of which are the ultimate answer to the problem. Hopeful measures, yes. In some instances, perhaps, last resorts. Open doors. But not the final answer. Is it any less reasonable to assume that heart transplantation, a far more formidable procedure than any surgical procedures on the heart which have preceded it, will require less time for a solution? It would seem not.

It seems that when one problem in this field is solved, others arise. For example, the recently heralded (and rapidly mushrooming) procedure of grafting a piece of vein between the aorta and a diseased coronary artery has more recently (and ironically enough) met with a mysterious and disheartening process of occlusion of the engrafted vessel in a high percentage of the grafts. Until the appearance of this nullifying process, this procedure held forth perhaps the greatest promise of any devised to date, at least for certain cases. But as fine a procedure as it is in selected cases, it has yet to prove itself in the crucible of time.

The sad fact remains that the prevention, or arrest, of coronary heart disease remains far superior to "cure" methods now at hand or available in the foreseeable future. Someday, it is to be hoped, this truism will be reversed. But when? A vis-a-vis confrontation with the fact that a vigorous, medically supervised, personal attack on the Big Three factors amenable to patient participation—diet, tension, and physical inactivity—offers the greatest hope for the greatest number of actual or potential coronary victims today. It is the first step toward individual, as well as collective, victory.

A few years ago, when in a quandary as to whether or not to submit to coronary arteriography,* I kicked around in my mind the problem of eventual surgery (if the X-Rays so indicated a need) for what seemed eons. I consulted with some of the best minds in medicine, and I meditated long and hard. And I prayed. When the answer came, it seemed very clear. It was no. And it was based, from a human standpoint, on the fact that even if arteriography had revealed coronary disease, I would do little or nothing differently. I had licked obesity, cholesterol elevation, and, to a large extent, tension; and I was capable of a high degree of physical endeavor, age and other factors considered.

* Coronary arteriography is a procedure whereby catheters are inserted into an arm artery and advanced to the base of the heart, opposite the coronary openings, whereupon dye is injected and rapid-sequence X-Rays and/or movies of the heart are taken to outline the coronary arteries.

What it amounted to, in the final analysis, was a choice of continued personal, vigorous, active attack on my problem—utilizing the concept of the Big Three—rather than resorting to the passive, leave-it-to-the-doctor approach. Thus far (after 9 years) I have not been sorry. And the longer I live, the harder I play and run, and the more I study the problem, the more convinced am I that I made the proper choice—or had it made for me by the Great Physician.

What's more, even if surgery had the pat answer to my problem this very day, for a way of life I would still elect the one I have found by the grace of God.

# CHAPTER VI

# A Bridge of Faith

New faith is the substance of things hoped for,
The evidence of things not seen.
                                    Hebrews 11:1

Having arrived, then, through much study and deliberation, at what seemed and what has since proved a logical approach to doing battle with the threat of a heart attack—prudent diet, anti-tension measures, and physical exercise in adequate amount—my most risky decision was yet to be made, to step up my exercise program to adequate levels.

Obviously, proper dieting entailed little or no risk. Neither did passive anti-tension measures, such as avoiding tension situations and relaxing whenever possible with good friends, good music, good literature, and the like. But the use of what would constitute a truly adequate exercise program, based on the then-available evidence (and as has since been shown to be the case), was fraught with an unknown amount of risk. Heretofore my exercise program had consisted of tennis played in somewhat random fashion, a program which was inadequate in the light of more recent studies. The injection of jogging, and eventually running, into the program, however tactfully done, theoretically could spell disaster—swift and final—to a man wearing a cardiac tag such as mine. The courses open to me were as follows: (1) Accept the advice of my cardiologist at face value and slow down my activity rather than step it up; (2) submit to coronary arteriography and probably find out for certain if and how much of a problem existed (and if so, then consider the possibility of some risky surgery *); (3) launch

* Personal communication with one of the nation's leading cardiovascular surgeons

into a stepped-up activity program on my own. Though possessed of the utmost respect for my cardiologist the first of these courses was distasteful to me for several reasons: It made me a cripple, a label I could not bring myself to accept. Moreover, with two small boys on the way up, I could not see myself having to refrain from participation in active play with them. I wanted to be a kid with them—to run, to play their games—simply because I felt this was one of the great thrills, if not a duty, of fatherhood, not to mention the image of "half a father" my sons would carry with them all through their lives.

The second course of action at the time carried about a 0.5 percent risk of death—one chance in two hundred that the diagnostic procedure would prove fatal.** Minimal, one would have to admit, unless that one happened to be you. The surgical risks were considerably higher even in the best hands—on the order of 10 to 20 percent, depending on the procedure.

The third course of action had by far the greatest appeal, primarily because if I could work into a good program I would be doing everything I could do to forestall a heart attack, regardless of what angiography might show. But there was a definite risk attached. Jogging and cardiac problems commonly did not mix, especially when the fitness program went unsupervised.

But one day, on my knees in prayer, I crossed a bridge of faith in Jesus Christ and reached a decision to put my trust in him and launch into a stepped-up program. My goal? To run one to three miles at least three or four times a week, a level of activity consistent with what seemed capable, at the time, of producing an optimal exercise response, and a level which has since been shown by authoritative sources to maintain a desired status of cardiopulmonary reserve.

Why the necessity of a bridge of faith? To offset the element of fear? Fear of the unknown? Fear of sudden death? To a degree,

at this point led to recommendation of immediate workup as a possible candidate for surgery.

   ** The risk of this procedure now is practically nil in competent hands.

yes. If you have ever, all alone, faced yourself with the intense question: "What would it be like to die suddenly?" you would know.

But more. More like the seeking out of an old Friend to travel with me down this unknown path, a Friend of Whom Paul Spoke: "I can do all things through Christ which strengtheneth me" (Phil. 4:13). *All* things. Weak and fearful and uncertain in my own flesh, I became strong and assured and confident with Christ beside me. Hesitant steps were made sure. The pounding heart and the breathless state that faced me in a run no longer filled me with dread. The worst that could happen to me, I knew, was to go suddenly into his Presence, and I came to be able to say with the great apostle: ". . . to die is gain" (Phil. 1:21), if that should be his will. In short, I have since come to realize that God gave me this bridge of faith not so much to help me with my misgivings as to strengthen my walk (or, to be more exact, my run) with him. Just to step out on his Word and say, "Thy will be done," was a great and thrilling experience I would not trade for all the gold in Fort Knox.

I had come to know Jesus Christ as a personal Saviour when a teen-ager, and I knew what a thrilling thing it is to walk with him. Early in my Christian life he had seen me through some mighty tough places, and out of habit, I suppose, I sought him out in my present task. Had I not wandered from his side along life's way; gone down into Egypt, as it were, disobeying his commandments and getting out of his will, I am certain that the physical ailments which had befallen me at a relatively young age would not have done so for many years later. For sin, aside from being a burdensome and exacting and wearisome thing, is a state of stress. And in me it had taken its toll and imposed an onerous burden over the years—emotional, financial, and physical. But Christ is a forgiving Lord, and with renewed allegiance to him I took my leave of relative inactivity and began my program in earnest.

Looking back now, I can see that my experience with the cardiologist was heaven-sent, and I praise God for it. For it has brought me back to a walk with him, and I am far richer now than I ever was before.

Obviously it would be possible to make such a decision as I did strictly on a human plane, without Jesus Christ. But I want it clearly understood that I did not come to faith in him through this episode in my life. Rather, as stated, my faith in him dated back many years. Yet it took this event to bring him *back* into my life. For while Christ is concerned with physical heart disease, he primarily is concerned with spiritual heart disease, and I devoutly believe that God may use the former as an instrument to cure the latter. Such was the case with me.

The important point here is that while my faith in Jesus Christ was the catalyst which made my decision to adopt a vigorous physical fitness program, the position in which I found myself was, I am convinced, of God's doing.

I would hasten to say that the Christian who finds himself in shoes similar to mine should not act carelessly—solely on the basis of one man's experience—for each individual is a different person. He should consult his own physician, and seek God in prayer for the solution of his own problem. The answer he receives may be quite different from mine. But I am confident, as is any true Christian, that the answer he receives will be the correct one, for our Lord has assured us that he answers prayer and meets our every need. He will never leave nor forsake us. His grace is sufficient for any situation.

To the unbeliever, the foregoing statements doubtless seem a mystery, or else the jumbled jargon of a frightened fool. Since it is beyond the scope of this book to defend the Christian faith, I will take the time here only to point out that Scripture clearly states that to the carnal man (the unbeliever) the spiritual man is a mystery; neither can he understand the things of the Spirit (1 Cor. 2:14). Faith in Jesus Christ is the door to such understanding, and no man can enter into the presence of the one true God by any other door (Jno. 10:9; 14:6). The first chapter of 1 Corinthians clearly explains that it has pleased God to use the foolish things of this world to confound the wise. Such truths defy logic and are therefore difficult for the proud of intellect to accept, for they are based on faith, without which it is impossible to please God (Heb. 11:6).

The Bible tells us that "faith is the substance of things hoped for, the evidence of things not seen" (Heb. 11:1). I never have encountered a better definition. The list of pragmatic examples of faith is endless. Faith in the law of gravity permits us to carry on our daily activities without fear of floating off into space; faith in a doctor permits restoration to health or prevention of disease; faith in an investment counselor permits hope of making a profit; faith an astronaut demonstrates as he climbs into a space ship and straps himself down for a trip to the moon allows him to place himself in the hands of countless technicians he does not know. We order mushrooms in a restaurant, knowing that the look alike toadstool is poisonous. In faithful anticipation, we flip a switch and a light comes on, the evidence of things (electricity) not seen. With perfect assurance someone stands before a cassette of film and hears a click and a whir, and a few minutes later sees X-Ray pictures of his chest, the evidence of things (X-Rays) not seen. The array of examples is endless.

The evidence of men's faith in themselves likewise is endless— that intangible assurance within one's own mind and body that a certain problem will succumb to the wholehearted onslaught of perseverance and confidence. There is a mighty ocean to be spanned with a cable, so that voices on one continent may converse with voices on another. The man who says it can be done is a fool; but Cyrus does it. He is a fool.

There is a way that man can fly like a bird. There is bound to be. But man is not made to fly. And so say hundreds of attempts lying in tattered ruins on the pages of scientific history. He never has, and he never will. So say millions more, faithless millions who have never tried, and never will. Fools, these Wright brothers. Fools with faith, the kind that sprouts wings in the mind, then on the ground.

There is a way that man can send his voice along a wire, across miles and miles and miles of far-flung countryside. Nonsense. Until a man wore out everything except his own faith and invented the telephone.

And light. There is a way that a man can turn back the darkness. There is bound to be. What fool says so? Thomas Edison says so, and again, everything but the man's own faith is worn down before the night is conquered once and for all. And space. Man can send his voice through space. How very foolish! Of course he cannot! Even if the waves, those unseen figments of the imagination that fill the void, are there, he cannot harness them. Absurd! Is it? Let us try, says Marconi. Let us have faith. And the radio is born. And television, and relativity, and atomic power, and computers, and space ships, and heart transplants, and artificial hearts.

All such very foolish things, until they are discovered, until they become reality, until a man—sometimes just one—is imbued with the spark of . . . faith! And then, how very real that faith! First a figment of the mind, then a spark of confidence that puts the flame to that figment, then . . . mountains move.

Faith! "The substance of things hoped for, the evidence of things not seen." Such a nebulous, foolish thing, says Mr. Pragmatist as he whooshes through the air at the speed of sound; while he watches a picture on a tube reaching him from halfway around the earth, as he talks to his secretary via radiotelephone hundreds or thousands of miles away. Yes, Mr. Pragmatist, such a foolish thing, this faith. Until it flies! Until it speaks! Until it leapfrogs space and lands on the moon! Until it becomes *reality!*

## Spiritual Faith

At the mere mention of spiritual faith, most unbelievers (and many professed believers) suddenly find reasons to make their exits, or else slam shut the doors of their minds. There suddenly is conjured up mental images of pulpits and pews, organ music and church steeples, black frocks and long, oak-bucket faces, tombstones and coffins, all glued together with an endless array of do's and don'ts.

None of these have anything to do with real spiritual faith. Quite the contrary! True faith in a risen Christ wears a splendorous robe of all the colors of the rainbow! It is springtime. It is Easter. It dazzles the mind's eye, as a field of mixed daffodils, bluebonnets, and winecups atop a thousand green-capped hills. It is music born of a heavenly chorus, too splendorous for the human ear fully to appreciate. It swells within the heart and bursts in a tumult of glorious counterpoint and melody.

The face of faith, though sometimes hidden by the more somber mask of flesh, is cherubic, rosy-hued, and full of laughter and mirth. It is devoid of tombstones and coffins and, in fact, its Author, Jesus Christ, is the only Person who ever lived on this earth who broke up funeral processions and turned tears of despair into tears of joy. What's more, the wonderful thing is that he still lives, and he still breaks up such processions; for the true believer never dies; he only moves on. True spiritual faith is full of life and peace and a new-found freedom from the awful slavery of sin. No church house, no casket, no cemetery, nothing that man has ever built, hewn, or devised can imprison it. It defies the boundaries of time and space. These are truths that, alas, none but the believer can know and understand.

Spiritual faith differs from materialistic faith in direction only, but not in quality. That is, faith remains by definition, in whatever realm, "the substance of things hoped for, the evidence of things not seen."

One may ask: what is the difference between faith and fantasy? And the answer is that faith is validated through fulfillment. It is belief with an unfolding future, while fantasy is but an impotent dream. Faith is a potent power that moves steadily, in totality and with force "from egg to fledgling to soaring eagle." Fantasy is but a punchless vision that dies a prisoner of the egg. Faith is hope empowered by a firm foundation, fantasy is a flight of thought with no launching pad, no power, and no flight plan!

Faith can build a bridge, land a man on the moon, or build an H-bomb, all of which represent faith in materialistic capabilities to give substance to things hoped for, things yet unseen. Such is the faith of materialism: the horizontally directed faith of man in himself, in mankind, in mind, in matter. It is the stuff which links his past to his present, his present to his future, one generation to another.

Spiritual faith, on the other hand, is directed toward God. It is vertically oriented, and looks upward to a higher Power and Source than flesh. It does not depend on man, but on God. It finds its fulfillment not in man, but in a transcendent, almighty, omnipresent, and omniscient God. Spiritual faith rises above mind and matter, and because it does it is incomprehensible to the natural man, just as the laws of physics are incomprehensible to the uneducated individual—not because they are any less real, but because they are beyond his ability to perceive (1 Cor. 2:14).

This is but another way of saying that God, because of his infinite complexity and greatness, defies the apperception of the human mind, which tends to run from that which it cannot fathom. Can a two-year old solve an equation in calculus? Can a toddler lay plans for a mighty skyscraper? Can a frog jump to the moon? or dive to the deepest depths of the great oceanic valleys? How absurd! Is not it, I ask you, just as absurd to expect the rational mind to be able to perceive the wisdom and the might and the power and the knowledge of an infinite God?

It is because of this very chasm between the mind of God and the mind of man that God has pointed out that we must come to him by faith, and that without faith it is impossible to please him (Heb. 11:6). The how of his ways, the why of them, the when and the where and the what of them are simply too vast, too complex for the tiny little computers that God has placed in the minds of men. "Oh the depth of the riches both of the wisdom and knowledge of God! How unsearchable are his judgments, and his ways past finding out! For who hath known the mind of the Lord? or who hath been his counsellor?" (Romans 11:33, 34).

No, excuses to reject Jesus Christ are easily come by. I know. I used a few myself before I accepted him, and even more when for years I left his side. The world is, indeed, too much with us. What is difficult is that first small act of faith to confess with the tongue and believe with the heart that Jesus is the Christ—the Son of the living God (Romans 10:9). But once that first small step is taken, the results are as miraculous as space ships roaring off of drawing boards, as one man's heart beating steadily inside the chest of another; as earth, viewed from the moon. "Behold, all things are become new—the old man is crucified with Christ" (2 Cor. 5:14; Rom. 6:6).

Accepting Jesus Christ at his word is comparable to boarding a plane for a distant destination. We are told that the plane is headed for a certain place. That is what itinerary, tickets, and the signs at the plane's point of departure tell us. It is going where we want to go. So with faith in a pilot we have probably never seen and do not know, and faith in the structural integrity and the engineering of an aircraft we have never laid eyes on before boarding, we board the plane, confident that it will carry us to our destination. We do not understand how several tons of metal can hurtle through space at speeds approaching or, in some planes, exceeding sound. We do not presume to fathom aerodynamics, jet engines, navigation. We simply accept, by faith, that this vehicle will get us where we want to go. Quite likely we are nervous and uncertain as we climb aboard, especially on a first trip. We can think of many reasons not to embark. But once airborne, how wonderful it all seems. And when we reach our destination our faith is vindicated. So it is with faith in Christ. Without that first step of faith, one will never know the thrill of knowing this wonderful Person, Christ the Lord.

Long ago, as a college student, I reached the inevitable conclusion that Christ could be only one of two extremes: (1) An insane bigot, a mad man, the greatest liar, magician, and con artist who ever lived, perpetrating on mankind the most stupendous fraud of all time, or (2) Precisely who he claimed to be—the Son of God, sent by the Father to perform a mission, the salvation of lost man; a Man capable of backing up his claims with the irrefutable evi-

dence of an empty tomb and the conversion of a handful of snivel-
ling cowards, his erstwhile followers, into a church body that defied
death and persecution to change the course of history for all time.
Consider the claims of this Man, and you will agree that he had
to fall in one category or the other:

"I am the door: by me if any man enter in, he shall be saved"
(Jno. 10:9).

"I am the bread of life: he that cometh to me shall never hunger;
and he that believeth on me shall never thirst" (Jno. 6:35).

"I came down from heaven, not to do mine own will, but the
will of him that sent me" (Jno. 6:38). And this is the will of him
that sent me, that every one which seeth the Son, and believeth
on him may have everlasting life: and I will raise him up at the
last day" (Jno. 6:40).

"He that believeth on me hath everlasting life" (Jno. 6:47).

"I am the resurrection, and the life; he that believeth in me,
though he were dead, yet shall he live: And whosoever liveth and
believeth in me shall never die" (Jno. 11:25, 26).

"I am the way, the truth, and the life; no man cometh unto the
Father but by me" (Jno. 14:6).

"If ye had known me, ye should have known my Father also,
and from henceforth ye know him, and have seen him" (Jno. 14:6).

"He that hath seen me hath seen the Father" (Jno. 14:9).

No man has ever put into words—nor can he ever—the sublime
power, the inner calm, the newness of life, that comes with knowing Jesus Christ; but I felt it of the utmost importance to refer to
it here in minor detail, for it is the essence of my story. Without
this personal faith in this Person, the rest of my experience literally
and figuratively would have died on the vine. I never would have
left the valley of doubt and fear and indecision for the mountaintop
of confidence. To him who is able to do all things well be the power
and the glory.

To be able to walk with him in quiet confidence—yea, to *run* with
him—required a renewal of my allegience to him from whose
presence I had wandered many years ago, like a wayward sheep;

to him who had never ceased to love and to seek me, and—through a questionably abnormal EKG—called me back to his fold. Such is the relentless and ceaseless and eternal love of God!

> Not what, but Whom, I do believe
>     That in my darkest hour of need
> Hath comfort that no mortal creed
>     To mortal man may give.
>
> Not what, but Whom
>     For Christ is more than all the creeds
> And His full life of gentle deeds
>     Shall all the creeds outlive.
>
> Not what I do believe, but Whom
>     Who walks beside me in the gloom
> Who shares the burden wearisome
>     Who all the dim way doth illume
> And bids me look beyond the tomb
>     The larger life to live.
>     Not what I do believe, but Whom
>     Not what, but Whom.
>
> John Oxenham

"For I know in whom I have believed" (1 Timothy 1:12).

## CHAPTER VII

# The Crossing of the Bridge
# (From Fear to Fitness)

Life is struggle,
And struggle is life,
And out of struggle comes life,
And out of life comes struggle—
As a cocoon issues out of a moth,
As a moth from out a cocoon.

It was the bridge of faith, as stated, that enabled me to cross from a state of transfixing fear and quasi-fitness to one of confidence and optimal physical fitness, a better state, physically, than I had known since the days of my youth.

It is one thing to acquire knowledge, and quite another to put that knowledge into action. My faith in Jesus Christ enabled me to give legs to what I had learned in my extensive reading and communications. Indeed, "faith, if it hath not works, is dead" (Jas. 2:17). But if one will pardon a jestful intrusion here, I at this point conjectured the distinct possibility that faith *with* works would become dead.

What I had learned was that the random tennis I had been playing was, though a fun thing and by no means bereft of physical benefit, not the ultimate type of physical activity for maintaining optimal physical fitness. The data being accumulated in this area at the time was relatively new, and much of it experimental.

I have presented the essence of this data in a previous chapter: that the foundation for a good physical fitness program must be based on a continuous, rhythmic type of endurance activity, such as running, jogging, swimming, or the like. So new was such material, in fact, that my book, *Prescription For Life*, published in 1966 and recounting my informational experience, though widely accepted in some circles, was viewed with much skepticism in others. Since its publication, however, a veritable avalanche of publications on the subject, particularly as it relates to jogging, has followed. Unquestionably the most widely known of these is Dr. Kenneth Cooper's *Aerobics* (and, more recently, the *New Aerobics* and *Aerobics for Women*), which works (among others) substantiate much of what I myself long before its publication, performed as an act of faith.

A jogger, then a runner, I was at length determined to become. What I had first to accept totally was the added risk of a heart so shorn of adequate blood supply that it could not meet the added demands of sustained, vigorous exercise. At worst, I risked precipitation of a heart attack, sudden death. At best, I chanced to improve collateral circulation to a threatened heart muscle and, in so doing, to lower my risk of sudden death and increase my chances of surviving an initial heart attack.

Having fully assessed the risk and set in the balance the potential loss against the potential gain, I launched my jogging (and eventually running) program solely on my own. I relied entirely on the will of my God as to its outcome.

Had it not been for my faith in a risen Christ, I assure you my plan never would have gotten off the pad. I would have lapsed into the rocking chair of doubt, of inactivity, and I fancy that I would have become a cardiac cripple, afraid of every call for the least exertion. I think that eventually I would have quit tennis altogether and come to rely solely on the pills my doctor had given me (and which, incidentally, I still have as a keepsake). How do I know? No signs stand out in such bold relief as those at a crossroads. I had to elect one route or the other. Oddly, when the time came for my final decision, all the quandaries which had plagued me melted away and the answer was clear as a mountain brook.

I have said elsewhere that the man who, setting out upon a journey into the unknown, says he has no fear is either an idiot or a liar. But it is one thing to succumb to fear, to be paralyzed by it, and quite another to fight back, to meet it on its own grounds; to become the aggressor rather than the defender. The real difference in bravery and cowardice is not the absence of fear in the former, but rather the coming to grips with it, whereas the coward is its cringing victim.

I once asked a young man if he were conscious of fear when, as a Marine in Vietnam, his unit was attacked by the NVA. His reply was, "I'd be a liar to say I wasn't." In that action he stood his ground, was seriously wounded, and almost lost his life. But in acting in the presence of fear he was a brave man. This man acted in response to long training, yet he was not immune to fear. Two of his unit were known to have deserted their posts in the same action, which is no indictment of the men involved, but merely a reiteration of what we all know. No rational man is immune to fear.

Acts of desperation (such as being cornered in a fight for life or death), and instinctual acts of bravery (such as a mother's rush into a burning building to rescue her child) aside, premeditated bravery or courage stems either from within or without.

That from within commonly arises from the faith of man in man (if none other than himself), or science (as in a doctor's medical knowledge or skill), and often carries with it a fatalistic attitude of bravado and reckless abandon. A man in my own situation, embarking upon the same course I did, but without faith in God, would illustrate such a courage. And there are many such men, whose actions have required no less courage, certainly, than my own.

But my own courage came from without—from a Higher Source—as I have stated; and conversely, such a courage is no less real or effective than that which comes from within. If two men scale a mountain peak, one with the aid of a rope, the other without it, is one any less brave than the other? One is more foolhardy, no doubt (the one without the rope), but no less courageous. If two astronauts blast into the heavens, one with God in his heart, the other without him, is one any less admirable than the other insofar as his courage is concerned? Obviously not. The old argument that one who requires God in his life reveals a weakness, that the church is an opiate for the infirm, is true only insofar as it can be shown that God is a figment of the imagination. To this Jesus Christ has put the lie, and the shoe is on the other foot—namely, that he who bases his courage on anything less than God will ultimately, in his self-immolation, prove himself to be a fool.

To the spiritually-oriented man, a person who embarks on a dangerous mission without God at his side is comparable to the man who goes up in a questionably sound aircraft without a parachute when one is there for the asking. "Aha!" says the unbeliever, "such courage is compounded of weakness. Such a man must have a crutch." Again, I say, if God be God, and Christ his Son, then 'tis not a crutch he carries, but a life preserver. And I would ask such an accuser if he would prefer to voyage on an ocean liner not equipped with lifeboats rather than on one so equipped.

Here, again, we enter into the realm of the believer vs. the unbeliever, and again I would remind that it is beyond the scope of this book to explore in depth the Christian faith. The effort of this book is rather, as previously stated, to depict what faith has done for one man confronted with a fearful and threatening situation, and what it can do for you in a similar one.

In essence, the thought I would leave with the reader is that *fear does not make one a Christian* (unless it be fear of God's wrath, fear of what eternity holds without God); but Christ can, and does, give the believer courage in times of need. For Christ is a Friend who never deserts us, and his Presence in time of danger, as well as in times of calm, is as real to the true believer as a life jacket strapped about the waist in a stormy sea.

Fear, then, was the stagnating inertia which I had to overcome to expand my fitness program along lines that seemed clear from my library and communications research, and faith in Christ was the force which enabled me to overcome it. One might deduce that I was a man sandwiched in between a fearful situation on either side—one who was "doomed if he did and doomed if he didn't." Quite true, but keep in mind that the stepped-up program was directed *against* the then-extant grain of medical practice.

To embark into an area as yet unproved, against specific medical advice, contrary to the majority medical practice of the day, on one's own and without benefit of constant medical supervision, might be termed by most physicians not only unwise, but downright foolhardy. It did not seem so to me, but rather the natural, almost easy (except for the work and sweat involved) thing to do. Such was the case, I am convinced, because it was God's will for my life. There is no other suitable explanation, for as we shall see in the pages just ahead, what then seemed irrational and unwise (when weighed in the light of acceptable medical practice of the day) has since been shown and is being shown, in many cases like my own, to be a rational procedure. This was a fact I had no way of knowing at the time, for the proof of the pudding was yet to be! Only God could have known, and in answer to prayer and meditation he directed my path according to his will, for he alone can wisely look into the future. Never in my life was Proverbs 3:5–6 more real to me than then: "Trust in the Lord with all thine heart; and lean not unto thine own understanding. In all thy ways acknowledge him, and he shall direct thy paths."

My faith first took shape as a shadowy figure in a sweatsuit alternately walking and jogging while traversing a one-mile circuit laid out around a neighborhood bevy of city blocks in the vicinity of my residence. The shades of night were chosen for the undertaking for a number of reasons: (1) It was a time of day which was for me relatively free from routine responsibilities, and which kept me from hurrying through my routine, a very essential element in the conditioning phase of any such program; (2) it was a time when the tensions of the day had completed their winding-up process, and therefore was an ideal time for unwinding before retiring; (3) it was a time relatively free from intrusion by the curious and the jesters.

The last of these factors, thanks to the very recent popularization of jogging through many excellent avenues—books and organizations such as those listed at the end of this chapter—now seems, I realize, of minor importance. But in the early sixties it was worthy of consideration, for a jogger in those days was an item of considerable curiosity and the target of all sorts of barbs, both physical and mental. Some of these, of course, still remain—e.g., dogs and hot-rodders. But even the hot-rodders now if not actually getting into the act, at least give the jogger a reasonably wide berth with their souped-up machines. The dogs? Well, they are ever with us, I suppose, particularly when one's jogging circuit is around neighborhoods or parks. Doubtless they still account, even now, for some of my better track times.

But originally even the adults in the neighborhood got into my jogging act by hurling from the yards or porches as I sallied by such little taunts as: "Hey, man, your wife after you?" Or: "He went the other way!" Or: "Watch out, it's gaining on you!" And so on. And kids would trot alongside me, jestingly inquiring, "Whose team you on?" "Need some joint oil?" Once an inebriated fellow in a sleek limousine curbed me and asked: "Say, fella, wha' cha tryin' t' prove?" Jestingly I replied, "I'm a quarterback for the New York Giants—just keeping in shape!" "Oh, I shee," he shrugged and hiccoughed as I jogged on off.

Such are the vagaries of night that still again I was the object of a bet between a man and his wife—he that I was an old guy trying to get in shape, she that I was a teenager trying to make the team. When one evening the woman bustled down her walkway and stopped me to inquire, I could see the chagrin creep into her face when she got a close look at my balding pate and my greying sideburns.

Such was the environment in which a jogger found himself in those days, and often even one's home provided no shelter from chiding remarks. A guy had to be something of a nut to be out at night running around the neighborhood, believe me. Often, indeed, was a prophet then without honor even in his own country. Comparatively speaking, the motivation required to stick with it in those early days was manyfold what it is today when jogging is an accepted leisure-time activity. This is why I am all the more convinced that my own motivation and strength came from without, from a Source higher than I. My own flesh was too weak, either to will or to do, to carry such an undertaking to its ultimate fruition, particularly in the face of such odds, both visible and invisible.

Though the visible odds—the taunting children, the quipping adults, and the barking dogs—were quite real and at times disconcerting, they nevertheless were as nothing compared to the invisible ones, the greatest of which were the doubt and the uncertainty born of fear. And if my fear had perchance lacked substance, other than the questionable EKG, at the time I began my program, it was not long in growing legs, the chief of which were pain, and subsequently extrasystoles (known to the layman as "flip-flops," "turnovers," or "extra beats") of the heart.

The pain, as the EKG, was (and still is) of the grey area type, which is to say that it was not typical of heart pain (angina *). My pain, though not classic, was most assuredly compatible with atypical angina, which can have even more ominous significance (as to extent of coronary involvement) than typical angina. The pain had several components, which over the years I have come to know as old friends. I can never predict which of the lot will show up when. Insofar as pattern is concerned, they make neither rhyme nor reason. One of my friends is located just beneath my left armpit, and has a mirror image on the inner aspect of my left arm. This little fellow has a way of being quite annoying and persistent, and usually is of a dull, aching quality. Another such friend chooses to make his presence felt by sharp, lancinating jabs of pain shooting around the left (and occasionally the right) side of my chest, and I have probably been jarred out of sleep more by this fellow than any other. I can say without equivocation that he has made me more familiar with the fifteenth chapter of 1 Corinthians

* So-called typical angina occurs behind the breastbone, is of a crushing or vise-like character, is brought on by effort or anger and relieved by rest.

than any of his stooges.

There is still another member of this villainous band which punches me in my belly, high up under my right rib-cage, with the same type of pain commonly found in gall-bladder disease.* Then there are pains down my arms, behind my shoulders (especially my left), and just to the right of my sternum (breast-bone) with occasional extension upward into my neck. EKG's taken during or shortly after such episodes thus far have shown no significant changes from the original odd pattern, and I suppose that had I not heard a very famous cardiologist once remark that any pain within two feet of the heart is heart pain until proven otherwise, I would be less inclined to take a dim view of my agues. Thus far, as I have stated, I have no way of anticipating these friends; they drop in any old time. But it does seem that excessive fatigue, whether physical or emotional in origin, may be a precipitating factor.

At the outset of my conditioning program, my friends' appearance shook me considerably, especially if they came on the scene during or shortly after exertion; but as my program progressed and my neighborhood circuit eventually became (as the walking segments were gradually eliminated) wholly a jog, then a run, I learned to live with them. Now, instead of their slowing me down by their appearance, they stimulate me to keep up the pace. In recent years a number of studies have been conducted by such outstanding cardiologists as H. K. Hellerstein, Cleveland, and John Boyer, San Diego, wherein subjects with known coronary heart disease are exercised under carefully supervised conditions. Many of the men in such programs have had heart attacks, and some have heart pain, or angina. The general impression, at present, is that exercise exerts a beneficial effect in many such cases, and that certain subjects can actually "run through" pain—i.e., continue to exercise until the pain disappears, and in some cases, in time, overcome it altogether.

* In early 1971 X-Ray examination revealed that I do have a gall-bladder problem.

I have witnessed well-documented evidence that this run-through phenomenon may be attended by EKG changes showing pathologic variations during the pain, which become normal as the exercise is continued and the pain disappears. As for that matter the literature is replete with cases of people who have sustained major heart attacks and gone on to become very adept distance runners, skiers, and the like; many such cases I have documented in *Prescription For Life*.

However, I would at this point hasten again to emphasize to the reader, certainly nowadays, that such a person should not exercise except under the strictest of medical supervision. In fact, the appearance of any pain in or about the chest during exercise is a sure warning signal to check with a physician at once. This being the case, you say, why did I, the writer, tend to ignore such pains? The answer is that I did not do so entirely; early in my conditioning period I had checkups fairly frequently, always with unchanged results; but the tests conducted were not the ultimate—namely, exercise stress testing to the point of submaximal or maximal tolerance, as is done in numerous cardiopulmonary laboratories all across the country today. There are other reasons—reasons of faith—that I did not pursue such testing further. Additionally, at the time I was passing through the pain barrier, coronary arteriography, in particular (among the most precise of the various methodologies at the time), still carried with it a quite respectable mortality rate. In essence, the algebraic sum of the *pros* and *cons* for or against my submitting to the more esoteric forms of testing was, at the time, somewhat on the *con* side.

Over the past few years, with refinements in technique and cumulative experience in numerous laboratories and clinics across the country, this sum has shifted definitely toward the *pro* side, and the day may arrive when logically I may be forced to submit to such procedures.*

Again, I would reiterate to the reader that *under no circum-*

* See Chapter 8—Bright Friday.

*stances* should he or she consider it a safe and medically sane or sanctioned procedure to ignore any type of pain in or about the chest, whether related to an exercise program or not, and under no circumstances should he attempt, where some doubt as to his physical condition exists, a "do-it-yourself" fitness program.

Complicating the aforementioned pain problem was the appearance on the scene, some two years after I began my program, of another prime purveyor of pain—gouty arthritis. This antique disease of bluebloods is a metabolic disorder due to a genetically transmitted enzyme deficiency, and is characterized clinically by swollen, tender, inflamed, and exquisitely tender joints. Commonly affecting the great toe, as depicted in archaic paintings of a red-faced, bulbous-nosed, obese boniface of a character sitting stiffly in a chair with his heavily-swathed foot elevated on an ottoman before him, the gout hit me in an ankle, which at first I thought was but a sprain picked up on the tennis court. At first but a painful annoyance, it awakened me one night by the sheer torment of the weight of bed clothes upon my ankle (typical of the exquisiteness of gouty pain), whereupon laboratory evidence and examination promptly revealed the elevated uric acid levels in the blood which attend the characteristically hot, swollen, red, and tender joints.

Control of this ailment nowadays is accomplished very nicely by medication, but inasmuch as gout may affect almost any joint of the body, this disease has served only to further complicate the pain picture. Moreover, it may make itself known in more insidious agues and algias which may be aggravated by exercise, and certainly is not calculated to aid and abet an exercise program.

Also, inasmuch as gout patients have a statistically higher incidence of coronary heart disease, gout has a more ominous significance to the coronary-prone individual than it does to others. One therefore can imagine the impact of this ailment upon me, earmarked as I already was for a heart attack. It was as though, while reaching for my exercise program life-jacket as I drowned in a sea of coronary-proneness, fate threw me an anchor instead—an anchor which threatened my ability to carry on with my program.

At this point, I felt very much like Job. After being shorn of his family and his fortune, he was handed a crop of devastating boils which threatened his life.

A time or two about there, I even felt like heeding the advice of Job's wife, "curse God and die." What had my faith gotten me? How is an already-crippled man to carry on when his crutch suddenly is jerked from under him? But I should have recalled the whole book of Job. God told him again and again: "Brace yourself and stand up like a man; *I* will ask (the) questions." Then Job's ultimate end was better than his illustrious beginning.

*For God has a purpose to those who trust him in whatever he metes out!* This was a lesson, a most difficult one, I had not fully learned. That the best was yet to come seemed preposterous to Job when his world had fallen down around him, but because his faith never wavered God brought him at length to a far better end than his beginning.

When ultimately I had licked my acute attack of gout, which took a couple of weeks of painful hobbling and set me back considerably in my conditioning program, I at length limped back onto the tracks and the jogging paths again. And for a time, resolute that I should not lose all the ground I had gained, I had the fight of my life on my hands, literally gutting it on ankles and knees that made me wince with pain on every step.

Often I encounter persons who throw in the towel on their physical fitness program before it is hardly begun, because of some minor discomfort such as a muscle soreness or shin splints. It is plain that such individuals never really determined to go through with their programs in the first place. For I am convinced that if the will to do is there, it will take far more than shin splints or a toe-ache to sideline the truly dedicated fitness participant. The chief ingredient of any worthwhile physical fitness program, I am convinced, is mental toughness.

Mental toughness is born of hard knocks, but its bedrock is absolute and unshakeable faith in one's undertaking. Without it the aches and the stiffness and the pains and the sweat will get you sooner or later.

Mental toughness has different source springs under different circumstances, even in the same person. In this instance, with uncertain pain plaguing me from head to toe, the jut of my jaw, signified a refusal to quit.

And that jutted jaw was provided by my personal faith in Jesus Christ. For I know myself too well. I'm no hero, as I've already stated, but something—no, Someone—kept me going, provided the balm for my pain and the reason for my existing. (I thought a good bit of the time, that existing was all I was doing.) And I assure you, dear reader, that it is only by God's good grace that still I am going or will continue to go, so long as it is his good will. I know that God knew if I ever stopped I would never start again, that I would only wither and die on the vine. The pains of gout and my unlabeled friends still visit me from time to time, though not so regularly as before. But now they only make me bite my lips and laugh beneath my breath, as all the while I give to God the thanks for his all-knowing love.

As I pointed out earlier there was yet another leg to my fear—extrasystoles (extra beats of my heart). Most people have experienced them at one time or another. Most such beats are not really extra beats at all, but rather premature ones. They are contractions of the heart which occur in advance of the time they normally should appear in the cardiac cycle. If they originate above the ventricle, they are not ordinarily serious. On the other hand, if they arise in the ventricle, they are much more likely to be (though not always) of serious import, especially if such beats (PVC's—premature ventricular contractions) occur in an older individual (over 40), or in an individual with other evidences of coronary heart disease. Such beats occurring in runs—two or more in a row—are particularly ominous if arising from the ventricle, since this signifies a highly irritable heart muscle, with increased susceptibility to deadly arrhythymias such as fibrillation, a state in which the heart muscle is totally desynchronized, such that the different muscle bundles which make up the heart contract individually and independently instead of in unison. The fibrillating heart, a totally ineffective pump incapable of sustaining life for more than a few minutes, has been aptly described as resembling a writhing bag of worms.

This other leg to my fear put in its appearance some three or four years after I first began my program. I shall never forget the first episode, which occurred one evening as I lay in bed reading. My heart suddenly thrust itself into my consciousness with a succession of close beats that reminded me of a closely caged rabbit thumping impetuously against my chest wall trying violently to escape. There was no pain, but I do recall taking a deep breath and jolting from a semireclining to a sitting position. I struck myself quite forcefully over my left chest with my clenched fist, an instinctual (though medically sound) maneuver. The run of beats ceased as abruptly as it had begun, but I slept poorly that night, I must confess, for here was still another bedfellow to add to my growing list.

And its meaning was as portentous as any of the others, if not more so, inasmuch as sudden death from coronary heart disease (which accounts for over half the deaths from this disease in many series) is commonly initiated by such arrhythymias. Ordinarily this intruder reminds me of his presence with but one extra beat and I shrug him off, but on rare occasions suspenseful successions of outlaw beats come along, such as I have described above, following which I am more than ever aware of my plight.

Attempts to trap these beats on an EKG, either before, during, or after exercise long were unsuccessful, so that it was uncertain whether or not they arise in the ventricle or above it. A scant few months ago one was trapped. It was of ventricular origin. Close successions of such beats is considered an ominous sign by most cardiologists, but sensible exercise programs have been shown to raise the threshold at which such beats appear, and thus improve the overall picture.

With my background, what would you surmise if you were a betting man? Briefly, review the rattlesnakes that have crawled into bed with me: a hereditary tendency to cardiovascular disease; once-elevated (only occasionally now) blood lipids; a hyperreactive blood pressure (a tendency to develop high blood pressure in tense situations); gout; atypical chest pain; and, finally, extra beats of the heart, not to mention my browknitting EKG. Each of these items is a road sign of coronary heart disease, and I am, as of this writing, little more than half a century old.

From time to time I attempt to step back and take an objective look at my situation, an impossible task for anyone. Why not, I say at times, throw in the towel? Why fight it any longer? Why not arteriography? Why not, if suggested, remedial surgery, and hang the risk? Up to now, the answer always seems to come back: Even with objective evidence of coronary disease by arteriography, would surgery be worth the still-considerable risk? What more could I, or more accurately would I, do than I am doing now? Able to run two to four miles at a whack in average times of 7½ to 8 minutes per mile, I still can enjoy three or four sets of singles tennis in 95 degree heat. I am capable of carrying a full practice load, of playing a quite enthusiastic afternoon of touch football with my boys and their friends, of swimming and water skiing, and of having a ball doing it, even with all my friends to put in an occasional appearance.

As of now I am a useful, active citizen, a husband, and a father, capable of fulfilling the obligations of each duty. What more could the more erudite procedures of medicine or surgery offer me at this time? Perhaps a bit later, when the walls have closed in a bit more. But now? Well, let's take a look.

First, consider arteriography, an X-Ray method that utilizes dye injection into the coronary arteries via a catheter inserted into and up an arm artery to the base of the heart. The mortality of this technique some years ago when I began my program was in the vicinity of 1 percent, is now closer to 0.1 percent, a rather negligible value. But, accurate as it is, it does not always tell the whole story, for even with wide open coronary vessels demonstrated by this method, the story of what transpires at the cellular level remains obscure. Heart attacks with totally patent coronary vessels are well documented. And if there is blockage, would any surgical procedure now available be worth the risk or improve my work ability? What's more, there is good evidence that if one can pass a maximal treadmill test (see next chapter), this proves him to be in as good (if not better) shape to beat the coronary clock than patent coronaries as demonstrated by arteriography.

Heart surgery? There are presently available numerous procedures to restore a blood supply to compromised heart muscle, none of them easy and none with truly astounding results when following a large series over a long period, or when comparing such with a group treated by intensive medical care alone. The literature and medical seminars abound with *pro* and *con* presentations which commonly pit the internist (touting medical treatment) against the surgeon (usually, but not always, for surgery).

The mere fact that such debates exist, with neither side clearly victorious, is in itself evidence of the highly unsettled nature of the issue. Operative mortality rates on surgical procedures for revascularizing * the heart are reported variously as ranging from a low of 5 percent to a high of 25 percent, depending upon the stage of the disease dealt with, condition of the heart at surgery, age of the patient, previous heart attacks, and so on.

Even the least of these rates is great enough to make the knowledgeable candidate sit up and take notice, especially when such all-important unknowns remain as the ultimate fate of jump grafts ** and the fate of patients undergoing such a procedure, the long-term results in terms of symptomatic patient improvement and longevity, and the comparative results obtained with expert medical management as opposed to surgery. Granted that there are bona fide candidates for such radical surgery (I am personally acquainted with several, all of whom have been greatly helped), the views of such stalwarts in the field—such as Dr. William L.

* Restoring blood supply.
** In this procedure, a length of vein, usually taken from the leg, is interposed between the aorta and the coronary artery beyond the point of occlusion.

Glenn, American Heart Association president and head of thoracic surgery at Yale University—must be respected until more critical evaluations are available. At a recent AHA meeting,[1] Dr. Glenn had this to say regarding the much-in-vogue jump graft for coronary artery disease: "There is no evidence as yet that the operation prevents myocardial infarctions or prolongs life. So far no operation to revascularize the heart has consistently met these requirements."

*Medical Tribune,* a medical newspaper that cited Dr. Glenn, went on to point out that he was joined in his views by AHA president-elect Dr. J. Willis Hurst of Emory University, and by a panel of interdisciplinary experts who held a press conference to drive home their plea. Says *Medical Tribune:* "They stressed that the graft failure rate has been about 14 percent at one year in most reported series and has gone as high as 30 percent in some, and that growing experience has thrown doubt on some indications and contraindications that seemed reasonable as recently as two years ago."

Here in Dallas, Dr. Maurice Adam, utilizing the jump graft procedure in a series of seventy patients, obtained relief of symptoms in 81 percent, a remarkable figure.[2] Seven patients, or 10 percent, died an operative death. Still another report by Dr. B. F. Mitchel, also of Dallas, reveals an operative mortality of only 3 percent, with excellent results in over 90 percent of the patients with coronary disease involving *only one or two* of the three vessels. With three-vessel disease, an operative mortality rate of 21 percent is cited. Thus the operative mortality in any given group of patients depends on a multiplicity of factors which, even in the best of hands, often leaves a great deal to be desired in terms of operative mortality and eventual (long-term) outcome.

Nevertheless, let it be fairly stated in defense of surgeons using this procedure that these men are working with high-risk patients in whom the mortality rate might be considerably higher without

[1] See bibliography, *Periodicals,* number 17, Dec. 8, 71.
[2] See bibliography, *Periodicals,* number 4.

the knife. As yet, the answer simply is not known. The mystery of the strange occlusive process which involves a high percentage of the engrafted vessels, improved selection of patients for the procedure, and the comparative fates of surgically-treated vs. medically-treated patients are but a few of the more prominent problems which must be solved before jump graft surgery can be put in its proper perspective. Should coronary patients be operated upon while still in generally good condition, while still active, while still capable? Some surgeons think so, that the mortality rates would nosedive considerably. Others, equally versed in the overall picture, do not agree. Who is one to believe? Where to draw the line? The jury, quite obviously, is still out.

Living with a problem such as mine is very difficult, at best, and at least a continuous fight. Whether the fight occurs at the dinner table (diet) or on the operating table is perhaps in the long run not so relevant as that one must fight. And for this ability, this resolve, I thank my God for Jesus Christ with each passing hour.

Yes, I have largely crossed, on a bridge of faith in Jesus Christ, a tumultuous sea of physical defeat and spiritual death, but the crossing has been no simple thing. It has been done by the grace of God, alternately on my knees and by the sweat of my brow, his Word eternally in my heart.

There have been, and at times still are, great hovering fogs of uncertainty and clouds of despair which descend upon me when I am visited by my numerous friends. But the farther I proceed from the side whence I came—the land of utter futility, without future and without hope—the less dense are the clouds and the more infrequent their gathering. The closer to the other side of the bridge of faith I get, the brighter shines the sun of God's love. And whenever I momentarily drop my head in dejection and would tumble into the waves below, I have only to look up—toward the approaching end of the bridge—and he is there, bidding me onward. Truly, Jesus never fails.

**Some Books to Read and Organizations to Contact on Setting Up a Physical Fitness Program**

## BOOKS

1. *Adult Physical Fitness.* U. S. Government Printing Office, Washington, D. C. 20402.

2. *Aerobics* and *The New Aerobics.* Kenneth H. Cooper, MD. M. Evans and Company, Inc., New York, N. Y. 10017.

3. *Jogging.* Bowerman and Harris. Grosset and Dunlap, Inc., New York, N. Y. 10010.

4. *Physical Fitness and Dynamic Health.* T. K. Cureton, PhD. The Dial Press, Inc., New York, New York. 10017.

5. *How to Keep Fit and Enjoy It.* Warren R. Guild, MD. Harper & Row Publishers, Inc., New York, N. Y. 10020.

6. *Prescription for Life.* M. F. Graham, MD. David McKay Company, Inc., New York, N. Y. 10017.

7. *Sports and Physical Fitness.* American Medical Association (Copyright 1970), 535 N. Dearborn St., Chicago, Ill. 60610.

## ORGANIZATIONS

1. Richard C. Steiner, MD, Mile-a-Thon International, 1720 Termino Avenue, Long Beach, Calif. 90804.

2. Gabriel Mirkin, MD, Run-for-Your-Life, 14411 Butternut Court, Rockville, Md. 20853.

3. William B. Bowerman and W. E. Harris, MD, Jogging Club, University of Oregon, Eugene, Oregon 97401.

4. Warren R. Guild, MD, Road Runners Club of America, 721 Huntington Avenue, Boston, Mass. 02115.

5. R. L. Bohannon, MD, National Jogging Association, P.O. Box 19367, Washington, D. C. 20036.

6. Kenneth Cooper, MD, Aerobics Institute, 12100 Preston Road, Dallas, Texas 75230.

# CHAPTER VIII

# Bright Friday

Out of Eternity
This new day is born.
Thomas Carlyle

In the first chapter I described that never-to-be-forgotten day in my life I have labelled Black Friday; that infamous day when I was officially pronounced to be a victim of coronary heart disease.

On yet another Friday—Bright Friday—my inverted T-waves were at length to be put under the microscope. For more than eight years, with a strength born of faith in Jesus Christ, I must have run at least 5000 miles.

On this particular Friday I was to take a treadmill test administered by a very eminent cardiac physiologist and a cardiologist. The treadmill test consists of walking on a moving belt at gradually increasing speeds until the subject's heart rate reaches near-maximum (submaximal) or maximum (maximal) levels for his age, or until some warning sign intervenes. If one is able to pass this test without signs of myocardial (heart muscle) ischemia (oxygen deficit), he can be reasonably assured that he has a quite capable heart, at least functionally.

In fact, this test is now considered by many top-flight cardiologists to be superior to coronary arteriography to determine the presence or absence of significant cardiac pathology (disease). One may, for example, have perfectly clean coronary arteries as shown by arteriography, yet be a victim of angina or even of a heart attack. The treadmill test in such cases may reveal a problem where arteriography does not. Conversely, arteriography may pick up diseased vessels or heart muscle not detected by the treadmill test. Obviously, the cleanest bill of health is one which sports both negative arteriography and treadmill tests.

Pessimist that I am ("Oh ye of little faith"), while walking down a gaily decorated esplanade (it was the week before Christmas) a day or two before the test, I thought to myself: *What a Christmas present you'll probably get—a bad report on a bum ticker.* Gloom pervaded. All was *weltschmerz.* The gay Christmas music may as well have been a funeral dirge.

But such is ever the case when the Christian fails to exercise his faith, as I still am prone to do. The faith that overcomes fear requires exercise of spiritual muscles (prayer, reading of the Word) just as physical strength requires the exercise of physical muscles. The everready Christian charges his spiritual batteries daily, feasting on the Word, staying in touch with God, yielded to his will. Failure to do so invites the invasion of all the disastrous emotions, of which fear is chief.

When the day and the hour for the test at length arrived, the treadmill assumed the same gruesome features as an EKG apparatus. For all practical purposes it may as well have been a truth machine done up in black crepe. From the strictly human standpoint, I did not really want to know the truth. Ostrich-like, I had buried my head in the grey sand between truth and fancy for a number of years, so why, I asked myself, should I voluntarily subject myself to the devastating possibilities of the treadmill, to the risk of being denied the very thing on which I had learned to lean so hard for so long—vigorous physical exercise.

But one lesson I had learned faithfully through the long years of trial: Never run from fear. To be afraid is permissible, quite human. But to run away, that is cowardly. And cowardice never will be the product of faith. Faith had carried me through too many long and weary miles in the years that had passed, and it would not, I knew, desert me when the chips were down.

So as I was taken through the preliminaries preparatory to the test, I let my mind recount some of the many promises of God that even the Christian is prone to forget when he is on the spot:

> Fear thou not; for I am with thee: be not dismayed; for I am thy God: I will strengthen thee; yea, I will help thee; yea, I will uphold thee with the right hand of my righteousness (Isaiah 41:10).

> Be strong and of a good courage (Joshua 1:6).

> I can do all things through Christ which strengtheneth me (Phil. 4:13).

> Be careful for nothing; but in every thing by prayer and supplication with thanksgiving let your requests be made known unto God. And the peace of God, which passeth all understanding, shall keep your hearts and minds through Christ Jesus (Phil. 4:6,7).

"Be careful for nothing: but in *every*thing"—in *every*thing—in *every*thing—yes, even a treadmill test! Just turn loose, and let God! The thoughts saturated my mind as the minutes ticked away before I stepped on the mill. (Truly in me God has done more with one of less faith than any believer I know. I am so glad that Christ said that we need no more faith than is in a grain of mustard seed to accomplish miracles through him, for that is about as much faith, in many of the crises of my life, as I have been able to muster.)

The taking of a treadmill test requires the attachment to the body of a number of electrodes from which wires run to complex monitoring equipment and an EKG machine. In some instances a mask is affixed to the face of the runner to permit measurement of oxygen consumption. All of this, of course, is preceded by detailed history, physical examination, blood analyses, and a resting EKG, so that by the time one is ready to climb aboard the mill he feels as if he has been prepped for a mini-space trip.

In my own case I felt as if I had been wired for the electric chair, for, as I told my examiner, I would much prefer the amputation of both legs to being taken off the active roster or having my physical activities drastically curtailed. Looking back, I see that the anxiety which clamored for supremacy within me was the result of a signal sin—that of taking my eyes off Jesus Christ.

Peter, when bade to come to his Master on the water, did all right until he took his eyes off Christ, whereupon he promptly sank. Such will ever be the case. Jesus does not desert us in time of trouble. Why are so many of us Christians empty-faithed, when our Master bids us simply to take him at his word? If only we would realize, accept at face value, that he is ever at hand to lead and direct us! All we must do is look to him. Simply trust him! He will do the rest. Jesus never fails.

This does not imply that everything always will turn out as we wish. Nowhere in his word does God promise this. In fact, he assures us that following him will not be easy. It is not a bed of roses, but rather a trail of thorns. Faith does mean, however, that whatever the trial, however deep the despair that may ensue, Christ will be with us. His grace will be sufficient. "I will never leave thee nor forsake thee" are not idle words, thank God! They are full of power, but they will pervade our beings only after we can learn to say with Paul: "God forbid that I should glory save in the cross of our Lord Jesus Christ" (Gal. 6:14). Not in self. Not in our possessions. Not even in whatever measure of health God has given for a season. But only in Christ! Then, and only then, is it "Katy bar the door!" for demon fear!

So it was with more than a modicum of fear and trembling that I stepped onto the treadmill and the test began—first a walk, a fast, long-strided walk; then faster, and faster, and faster, until I ran. First the breathing coming easily, then more laboriously; heavier, harder, heavier, harder, until at length a heaving of the chest. First the heart beat relatively slow; then faster and faster, even faster, pushing with each swift minute toward a peak rate. First the coolness of the room; then the pleasant warmth of action; then blood heat; then drenching sweat.

To stay on a treadmill it is necessary to look straight ahead; but I was all too aware of my heart-tracing flicking across the oscilloscope, the intermittent whir of the EKG machine, the interval recordings of blood pressure, the measured monotone of my examiner as he would lend encouragement and mark the passage of precise time intervals. "You're looking good." "Coming up on ten." So many things were happening simultaneously that as the pace of the test quickened I found myself thinking of the Lord Jesus, and, strangely, there on the mill, my fear disappeared. The test, I am happy to say, went on to a happy and successful conclusion. But somewhere in the midst of it I knew that whatever the outcome, whatever the verdict, all was well, for Jesus, my Lord, was with me, and God's will was suddenly my will, and, when all was said and done, that's all that really mattered. Long before the test was over, I had said simply: "Lord, Thy will be done." And all was well. I was prepared for any eventuality.

The official report of the examiner read:

(1) Nonspecific T-wave changes, probably a normal variant.

(2) No signs of ischemic coronary disease.

Far better than I had first hoped for. But no more, I assure you, than my God can do!

What, exactly, was the significance of the favourable outcome of the test? Did it mean that the inverted T-waves had always been non-specific red herrings, not indicative of coronary heart disease at all, that there had, indeed, been much ado about nothing? Or did it mean that, through my physical fitness program, collateral circulation to my heart muscle had formed in adequte quantity to carry blood to once oxygen-impoverished areas? Or did it mean that God had himself done a bit of heart surgery in answer to prayer? (And I must here interdict that I never sell God short any more. He can do any and all things! In my book, as in his, he is omniscient and omnipotent, without limitation.)

I do not know the answer to the above questions. No one does. To be sure, there are esoteric methods of having known, had they been instigated from the outset. But at the time, as previously pointed out, seemingly unnecessary risk was involved. Moreover, so say the authorities, further searching is not indicated at this time.

And in the final analysis the answer is really unimportant. What was and is important is that in the eternal scheme of things God used an inverted T-wave on an electrocardiogram to bring home a prodigal son. The eternal scheme. This is what counts.

And if we can only remember that while we see what often appears the bleak side of the picture—the underside, the temporal —our God sees the heavenly side, the eternal. Furthermore, we are allowed but glimpses of the whole, while God sees the entire panorama of our lives at all times. How comforting it is to know that "our light affliction, which is but for a moment, worketh for us a far more exceeding and eternal weight of glory; while we look not at the things which are seen, but at the things which are not seen: for the things which are seen are temporal; but the things which are not seen are eternal" (2 Cor. 4:17,18).

> My life is but a weaving
> > Between my Lord and me,
> I cannot choose the colors
> > He worketh steadily.
> Ofttimes He weaveth sorrow,
> > And I in foolish pride
> Forget He sees the upper and I, the underside.
> Not till the loom is silent
> > And the shuttles cease to fly
> Shall God unroll the canvas
> > And explain the reason why.
> The dark threads are as needful
> > In the Weaver's skillful hand
> As the threads of gold and silver
> > In the pattern He has planned.

Ah, yes, when we can see things through the eyes of God, through the eyes of faith, black becomes white, night becomes day. For the long look of God sees beyond the dark valley of the here and now to the mountain peaks far above, bathed in the splendor of eternal sunlight.

I had a glorious Christmas that year. From the middle of my

treadmill journey, when my faith again reached up, I have never ceased to thank him: Not alone for the seeming reprieve he has so graciously given me to be with my young sons for yet a little season in the capacity of an active father rather than an incapacitated, half-alive cardiac cripple; but more for one more finite glimpse of his infinite love and care. He cares for me. He gave his only begotten Son that I might be his adopted son. He sent his Son, a Lamb without blemish, to die in my stead; for me, a sinner, condemned, unclean. What love! What infinite love!

God's infinite power indeed is awesome. Roll all the H-bombs now in storage into one and they would be but a grain of firecracker powder compared to his infinite power. But spellbinding as this is to contemplate, his mercy and his love are what enthrall me even more. That he Who spake the universe into being, he Who was in the beginning and evermore shall be, even from everlasting to everlasting, should care for an insignificant bit of sinful flesh such as me—first to grant me sonship in his kingdom through his only begotten Son, when I was but a youth; then to recall me when, years later, I had wandered far from his fold. To love the lovely— that is so easy. That is human. But to love the unlovely. That is so difficult. That is God. And to give One's only Son, a Son without blemish or fault, to die for all that he abhors, for all that is a noisome stench unto his nostrils, for *all* that is evil and corrupt and vile and debased! Well, that is impossible to man. But not to God! For God is perfect love. And perfect love casteth out fear. And that is why fear cannot live in the same mind where Christ is King. Because Christ is the Ambassador of Perfect Love, in whom is our peace and our security forever and ever!

On that Black Friday of many years ago, I wanted so to die. All was dark, foreboding, full of death. I was far from my Father's arms. But this bright Friday on the mill I was full of life. And had I died in my tracks I would have been just as alive in him. At the end of that second Friday, how wonderfully and joyfully at peace with my God was I!

Once again, I see now, God had tested my faith—such a weak

and unstable thing—yet just enough to prove his mighty word. "Prove me and see—" Once again he had directed my path, through a most unlikely set of circumstances not of my own doing, to the treadmill, there to let me know even more that he is a sovereign God, One who not only saves us, but keeps us day by day, step by step, down each weary mile.

Never in my wildest dreams did I think that I would praise my God for sending into my life such an array of disasters and obstacles. But now I can see that it has all been but a part of his plan for my life, a plan that included a crazy T-wave to call me back to him. Trial and tribulation, when one is in the will of God, are but whetstones that sharpen our faith and remove the rough edges, fires that melt out the impurities, pressures that conform us more toward his image.

In this, his process for making diamonds from coal, he spared not his own Son, so that Christ might in his humanity come fully to experience the lot of fallen man, though there never was any imperfection in Christ. Hebrew 2:10 tells us: "For it became him, for whom are all things, and by whom are all things, in bringing many sons unto glory, to make the captain of our salvation perfect through sufferings."

Horatius Bonar expressed the value of strife quite eloquently:

> Great truths are greatly won. Not found by chance,
> Nor wafted on the breath of summer dream,
> But grasped in the great struggle of the soul,
> Hard buffeting with adverse wind and stream.
> Grasped in the day of conflict, fear and grief,
> When the strong hand of God, put forth in might,
> Plows up the subsoil of the stagnant heart,
> And brings the imprisoned truth-seed to the light.
> Wrung from the troubled spirit in hard hours
> Of weakness, solitude, perchance of pain,
> Truth springs, like harvest, from a well-plowed field,
> And the soul feels it has not wept in vain.

I cannot know (nor would I will it, if I could) what lies around the next bend, over the next hill, of life. Each of us lives "in the middle of a moment, somewhere between the cradle and the grave." No man can buy a lease on tomorrow, even though his wealth may stagger the imagination. Neither wealth nor fame can stay the scythe when a man's number comes up.

How many men I have known, many of them wealthy, who have boasted of tomorrow. "Tomorrow I will do such and such." "Next year—" "When my kids finish school—" But God has said: "Boast not thyself of tomorrow; for thou knowest not what a day may bring forth" (Prov. 27:1).

The Bible tells of such a boaster, a wealthy man who was so rich he declared he would tear down his barns and build larger ones, where he could store all his worldly possessions. "Soul," he told himself, "thou hast much goods laid up for many years; take thine ease, eat, drink, and be merry" (Luke 12:19). But God called him a fool. Why? Because that very night his soul was required of him. He had provided for his earthly needs, but he had neglected to make provision for eternity, for God.

The natural man often is so preoccupied in providing for his flesh, accumulating the stuff of this world, that he digs for himself an early grave. But God hath said: "a man's life consisteth not in the abundance of the things which he possesseth," and again: "Lay not up for yourselves treasures upon earth, where moth and rust doth corrupt, and where thieves break through and steal: But lay up for yourselves treasures in heaven, where neither moth nor rust doth corrupt, and where thieves do not break through nor steal" (Matt. 6:18,19). For: "What is a man profited, if he shall gain the whole world, and lose his own soul? or what shall a man give in exchange for his soul?"

Indeed, how frail is life! How thin the line between life and death: but the length of a heartbeat, the tick of a watch, the thickness of a scalpel's edge. The Bible puts that frailty in best perspective when it asks: "What is your life? It is even a vapour, that appeareth for a little time, and then vanisheth away" (Jas. 4:14). Again, it tells us that "all flesh is as grass, and all the glory of man as the flower of grass. The grass withereth, and the flower thereof falleth away" (1 Peter 1:24).

Indeed, the sober-minded man must ever remember the words of the Psalmist, when he said: "Lord, make me to know mine end, and the measure of my days, what it is; that I may know how frail I am. Behold, thou hast made my days as an handbreadth; and mine age is as nothing before thee; verily every man at his best state is altogether vanity" (Ps. 39:4,5).

Often, in periods of quiet meditation, I sit mentally aghast at the swift passage of time, the quiet and ceaseless trek of the years. Only yesterday, it seems, I was a barefoot boy roaming the fields with my dog and my gun. Today I am well over the top of life's mountain. Yesterday my little boys were cozy little bundles of warmth snuggled in my arms. Today they stand almost shoulder to shoulder, eye to eye. Can we pause long without hearing the poet's sage observation?

> Earth turns.
> Seasons roll,
> And time moves like a wraith from pole to pole—
> Turning the leaf, paling the rose,
> And etching footprints on the face of those
> I know—and love—and would not bid adieu!

Someday, somewhere, perhaps soon, I know I shall run my last mile. It may be tomorrow. It may have been today. On the day's clock of life none of us can know whether we live in the dawning or at a quarter to midnight. None of us can say *wie viel uhr es ist* —what time it is.

I have seen newborn babes the picture of robust health one day and in a casket the next. I have seen men of all walks of life and at all age levels—some prominent, some wealthy, some their cheeks blushed with the rose of youth, others their hair frosted heavily with hoary grey—go suddenly and without warning into eternity. Some were ready. Some were not. But dust must to dust return, and ofttimes quite unexpectedly. Are you, dear reader, ready for such an event?

It is very wonderful to know the eternal God, who so loved us that through Jesus Christ he has conquered death, for whosoever will believe. That's good news. That's very wonderful. That gives confidence for living, one day at a time. That stretches all our tomorrows out into infinity, so that at times I find myself rather homesick for heaven. Only in recent years have I come to know what Paul the great apostle had in mind when he said that "to die is gain" (Phil. 1:21), and when he spoke of "having a desire to depart, and to be with Christ" (Phil. 1:23), "willing rather to be absent from the body, and to be present with the Lord" (2 Cor. 5:8). Faith in Christ not only conquers the fear of death. It conquers death itself. Thus can the Christian, in the words of Paul, literally scoff at death: "Death is swallowed up in victory. O death, where is thy sting? O grave, where is thy victory? . . . Thanks be to God, which giveth us the victory through our Lord Jesus Christ" (1 Cor. 15:54,55,57).

And so I thank God for the Fridays—the black and the bright —in my life. Though at times they seemed insurmountable obstacles, I see now that they were of his making. Building blocks of faith they were, and I have come away from them a stronger and a better Christian.

If it pleased God to make the Captain of our salvation, even Jesus, perfect through sufferings (Heb. 2:10), then should we, his adopted children, desire any less? Should not we rather thank him for the afflictions he sends to try us and to perfect us, to whet away the rough edges and mold us in the image of Christ? Indeed doth "our light affliction, which is but for a moment, work for us a far more exceeding and eternal weight of glory" (2 Cor. 4:17).

Just think! Without those T-waves I might still have been in a pigsty eating spiritual cornhusks in a distant land instead of enjoying the fruits of my Father's table. My eternal thanks to him for all my Fridays—and all the days in between! As M. D. Babcock has so well reminded us: "Some views of life are never understood except in review. Reserve your judgement, time will vindicate God, and if it does not set you singing, eternity will."

CHAPTER IX

# Across the Bridge

That I may tell pale-hearted fear it lies,
And sleep in spite of thunder.
Shakespeare *(Macbeth)*

Across the bridge of faith I have found a totally new approach to life, a new concept of living. Actually, this concept of total fitness is not a novel or a new one by any means, but ofttimes it is only after it has filled some great need in life, as in my own case, that it becomes crystal clear.

The concept embraces the realization that man is indeed a three-dimensional organism—body, mind, and spirit—and that any life which fails to recognize this truth will, when the chips are down, be faced with an insoluble dilemma. I shall here point out how my own experiences as I crossed the bridge affected me in each of the realms of fitness—the physical, the mental, and the spiritual. Perhaps comparisons of the before and after type may afford some illustration of the changes effected.

*Physical Fitness*

As I have indicated previously, my physical status prior to institution of my conditioning program was one of those *quasi* states somewhere between minimal and maximal (for my age and physiologic capacity). I played tennis with some regularity, and my weight was not entirely out of bounds, but I certainly had not reached my potential, either by subjective standards or by those so clearly outlined in any number of excellent works on aerobic exercise.

Here, in tabular form, is a fundamental comparison of my before and after status of physical fitness:

### Subjective Phenomena *

(1 to 4 scale = mild to severe, or poor to excellent)

|  | Before | After |
|---|---|---|
| General alertness | Poor—2 | Good—4 |
| Fatiguability | Easy—4 | Much reduced—1 |
| Insomnia | Common—4 | Occasional—1 |
| Irritability | Marked—4 | Minimal—1 |
| *Joi de vivre* | Occasional—1 | Often—3 |
| Optimism | Little—1 | Much—4 |
| Self-confidence | Poor—1 | Very good—4 |
| Tension feelings | Marked—4 | Low—1 |

### Objective Parameters

|  | Before | After |
|---|---|---|
| Avg. resting pulse rate (beats/min.) | 80–90 beats/minute | 48–60 |
| Avg. peak pulse rate (during sustained 20-min. run) | 200 beats/minute | 160–180 |
| ** Pulse recovery time | 2–3 hrs. | 2–3 mins. |
| Avg. resting blood pressure | 140/86–90 mm. Mercury | 120/72 |
| Blood cholesterol | 270–310 mgs.% *** | 190–250 |
| Weight | 160–165 lbs. | 140–145 |
| Waist measurement | 34–36" inches | 32–33" |

It should be obvious at once that the physical, and therefore the physiologic, effects of exercise have proved nothing short of phenomenal in my case. In the relatively short space of some three months, I would estimate, I underwent a metamorphosis from a sluggish, reluctant-to-live, overweight, hyperreactive, woefully inept physical specimen to an alert, eager, trim, reasonably calm, and able physical performer (considering age and physical capability) with a presentable level of serum cholesterol, a blood pressure stabilized within normal limits, and a markedly reduced resting

* Some of these phenomena spill over into the mental realm, illustrating the close intertwining of mind and body.

** Time required for pulse to fall from peak exercise rate to below 120 beats per minute.

*** mgs.% = milligrams per 100 cc. of blood. One milligram = 1/1000 of a gram, and about 455 grams = 1 lb. A cc. = a cubic centimeter, or about 1/1000 of a quart.

pulse, peak exercise pulse, and pulse recovery rate (indicative of the greatly increased efficiency of my cardiovascular system).

The sum total of this experience is that life is far richer and better and more abundant than in my previous state. Whether or not years will be added to one's life because of physical fitness programs is not yet medically certain, but it is an established certainty that, in most instances, such programs will add life to the years that one does have. Even were it a known fact that physical fitness adds naught to longevity, I would count not a single moment given to physical endeavor lost or wasted. The subjective improvement alone is worth every ounce of effort.

Consider, for example, fatiguability. Who would argue that ability to work for longer periods while feeling up to the task at hand will add productivity and enjoyment to one's labors? The returns on such an investment are thus identifiable not only as bodily rewards, but in monetary gain as well. In short, it is good economics.

Or insomnia. How many testimonials I have heard for sounder sleep resulting from a physical fitness program! How could one help feeling better if he experiences this effect?

Or irritability. If you're not winning any popularity contests among friends, try a fitness program and see if you don't become better company. I have numerous testimonials in my files as to this effect on participants in fitness programs.

Self-confidence? Optimal physical fitness adds immeasurably to positive feelings about one's capabilities in any undertaking. A body capable of reaching known physical heights likewise is capable of sustaining higher levels of mental and spiritual fitness. Paul, in fact, compares spiritual competence to physical competence, as in the running of a race (1 Cor. 9:24,25), and it is perhaps of more than passing significance that Christ chose physically capable men (when one considers their rigorous occupations and/or trials and tribulations) as his disciples. The Scriptures leave little room for doubt that Christ himself was a magnificent physical specimen, capable of the most arduous physical feats.

And under the influence of a proper physical fitness program, a Gloomy Gus commonly becomes a Glad Guy. Nothing de-monotonizes an otherwise drab and dull day like physical endeavor.

Perhaps most important, from the standpoint of coronary heart disease, is the effect of exercise on tension. The physiologic aspects of the relationship have been reviewed elsewhere. Here I would simply like to point out that as one learns to distinguish physical fatigue (long hours, no sleep, whose prescription is rest) from tension fatigue, characterized by a wound-up feeling, tension insomnia, and resting pulse rates faster than usual, he learns that physical endeavor is a tension-fighter supreme. How often have I experienced that done-in feeling so characteristic of tension fatigue, and, after forcing myself onto a tennis court or track, come away feeling completely rejuvenated. I am on firm ground, I feel certain, when I say that in combating tension fitness programs are without peer.

Now were such feelings my experience alone, then perhaps they would mean little, except to me. But testimonies by the thousands to the same effect are easy to come by. I have in my files numerous letters from people of all ages and all walks of life extolling like benefits from a physical fitness program, and I could list equally as many who have given similar testimony in verbal fashion.

Vigorous musculoskeletal action is the voice of vital body machinery. To ignore its clamor for expression is to ignore a sizeable portion of one's physical self. When one has reached the point that I have in incorporating fitness into his daily life, to miss this exhilarating portion of life experience is as memorable as forgetting to brush one's teeth, or to partake of daily bread.

True, subjective phenomena are difficult, if not impossible, to quantitate or qualitate in the laboratory; but such mass testimony to these effects cannot be totally ignored, any more than can, say, the feeling that an auto runs better when in good repair than when in a run down, neglected condition.

One will recall that improvement in objective parameters points to a more efficient cardiovascular and oxygen utilization system and reduced tension, all compatible with movement away from factors predisposing to heart attacks. Even if such improvement does no more than to improve one's chances of surviving his first attack, it is worth the cost in time and effort.

I can assure you that awareness of heart disease, whether the dawn comes in an oxygen tent or through routine physical examination as it did in my own case, is oft a blessing in disguise. It gives stimulus (and how!) and precious time for attention to one's state of fitness, both physical and spiritual, as well as to business matters ofttimes left with untied ends. A reprieve, a second chance, is worth a great deal. That no one can deny. For out of the clouds of gloom and doubt and fear can blossom the sunshine of a new way of life, often far better than the old one left behind.

*Mental Fitness*

To deal with mental fitness in depth would require many more pages than are here available. Suffice it to say that the functional interrelationship of mind and body has been well documented. The remarkable correlation of physical fitness and mental status was demonstrated notably in a study of West Point cadets a number of years ago,* and has been substantiated by numerous similar studies since.

Former President John F. Kennedy voiced a great deal of savvy of this fact when he once said:

> No matter how vigorous the leadership of government, we can fully restore the physical soundness of our nation only if every American is willing to assume responsibility for his own fitness and the fitness of his children. If we are to retain . . . freedom, for ourselves and for generations yet to come, then we must be willing to work for the physical toughness on which the courage and intelligence and skill of men so largely depend.

Through the President's Council on Physical Fitness, great

* As referred to in: *Hypokinetic Disease,* H. Krans and W. Raab (Springfield, Illinois: Charles C. Thomas).

strides have been taken toward upgrading the woeful status of fitness in American youth.

Again, in my own case, a comparison of before and after status of several aspects of mental fitness are in order:

|  | Before | After |
|---|---|---|
| Mental acuity | Dulled | Heightened |
| Reading speed | Comparatively slow | Markedly increased |
| Retentive power | Reduced | Enhanced |
| Inititative | Poor | Increased |
| Learning ability | Reduced | Enhanced |

Obviously such a comparison at best affords only a rough index of progress in but a few of the various areas of mental fitness. Even so, what is important is that there is a definite and decided improvement in mental status as a result of physical conditioning. Although such results hardly can be weighed statistically, they nevertheless cannot be totally ignored, particularly in view of the fact that more objective evidence of such improvement, as presented above, is available.

Increased awareness of the environment, heightened perceptivity, sharper wit, improved perspicacity, and smoother function of all mental processes all add up to a big plus factor for physical fitness totally unrelated to life span. Such physical fitness again, manifests itself not only in personal satisfaction, but in economic and social benefits as well.

The Greeks, ahead of their time, knew all too well the mental rewards of physical fitness. This is one reason they excelled in so many fields of mental as well as physical activity, and renders much of their philosophy self-explanatory. Sound mind in sound body rings not only of the complementary relationship of mind and body (psyche and soma), but of the mutual dependence of one on the other.

Undoubtedly, if physical fitness were more universal a practice in our nation, mental health would be less than the number one health problem it is today. The picture of rising suicide rates, wanton murder, rapine, and the skyrocketing rise of crime in general, not to mention mental cases filling more hospital beds than any other single ailment, is a morbid one, at best.

While such is not a matter of mind alone (for the spiritual portion of man is the fundamental fault in most problems of this type), nevertheless mental fitness, in turn largely revolving about physical fitness, plays a tremendous role. If sound bodies do indeed contribute to sound minds, then conversely sick bodies contribute to sick minds. There is little doubt that the physically fit person is better equipped to withstand psychic stress and trauma than the unfit.

The damning emotions of fear, depression, hostility, and rage, to name but a few, all root factors in mental illness and crime, find surprising outlet in vigorous physical endeavor. I suspect that if our nation as a whole pursued vigorous physical fitness with the same ardor that we play the role of spectator, we could close down many mental hospitals and as many jails. Here, again, physical fitness is not to be construed as the total answer, and it would be absurd so to contend. But that it plays a decisive role in mental fitness is beyond question.

## Spiritual Fitness

A 72-year-old man once ran ten six-minute miles per day, each day of his life, won numerous Boston marathons, and was in general a superb example of physical fitness. But a few years ago Clarene Medwar died, not of heart disease, but of cancer.

A long-time editor of a physical fitness publication, as able a performer as an expositor of physical fitness, had for years run several miles daily. But one day while on the second leg of his cross country journey, he fell to the ground and never got up, purportedly a victim of a deadly arrhythmia of the heart secondary to badly diseased coronary arteries.

Over two years ago, my medical partner of 17 years, a young man of 43, dropped dead in his tracks while doing his two mile jaunt around a park behind his home. He, along with me, had practiced physical fitness assiduously for many years and had passed a complete physical examination but a scant two months before his untimely tragedy.

The literature is filled with examples like this, and I could not even attempt so much as simply to list them here. I cite such cases but to raise one question: When a man, physically fit or otherwise, falls to earth never to rise again, *Is that all there is?*

A few years ago, a popular song asked that question. And in it the singer, recounting first one and then another joy and/or tragedy which she had experienced down through her life, asked, at the end of each, this portentous question: Is That All There Is? What a question! How staggering its import! Are we to say of life that physical fitness or mental fitness, a full and enjoyable three-score-and-ten, is all there is? The singer of the song concluded that if these life experiences are all there is, then let's bring out the booze and have a ball. A sobering question with a not-so-sobering answer, and yet a question which every man and woman must answer sooner or later, regardless of his or her state of physical or spiritual fitness.

There is no such thing as immunity to physical death. "For it is given unto man once to die." A man may run thousands of miles in his lifetime, but he cannot outdistance death. A man may, through a tremendous physical fitness program, feel that he has a new lease on life; but no amount of effort, no amount of where-withal, ever can buy a lease on eternal life. He may eventually be able to gain a number of months, perhaps years, through an artificial or transplanted heart; but sooner or later dust must to dust return. There is a mile common to every man, and that is the last one!

So let me again pose the question, dear reader, as one individual to another, physically fit or not. After you have played your last game of tennis, run your last mile, pedalled over your last hill, *is that all there is?* There are three commonly used avenues for dealing with this question. One is that of the stoic, who, as the captain of his soul, goes bravely down with his ship, having naught but his hollow belief in himself to go with him. Another is that of the

Epicurean, who takes the route of the singer of the song afore-mentioned, and through drink or drug or allied means escapes into the limbo of unreality. Still a third is he who puts his faith in other men, in the god of science, and, denying death unto the bitter end, staunchly believes that somehow man's knowledge will rescue him from the grave.

But I would remind you of yet another answer to this vital question, and that is the one provided by Jesus Christ, who said: "I am the way, the truth, and the life—he that believeth on me, though he were dead, yet shall he live" (Jno. 14:6 and Jno. 11: 25—free trans.). "And whosoever liveth and believeth in me shall never die" (Jno. 11:26).

No man is truly fit to live to the ultimate until he is fit to die, and I submit that no man is fit to die unless he is prepared to meet his God. There is only one door to God, and that is Jesus Christ: "I am the door" (Jno. 10:9). This door is entered by faith, simple faith, and faith alone, for "by grace are ye saved through faith; and that not of yourselves: it is the gift of God: not of works, lest any man should boast" (Eph. 2:8,9). It is a door not to be entered by turning over a new leaf, joining a church, reading the Bible, or having Christian parents, among other things. It is a door entered by simple, child-like faith in Jesus Christ.

The man who waits for all the answers to all the questions, who would reason his way to God is, alas, knocking on the wrong door. He will only wind up with a god of his own creation, and that is not God. Faith comes *first,* knowledge later. And truly it is amazing how the answers do fall into place after one becomes a member of God's household, an adopted son, through a simple act of faith.

Spiritual fitness begins with being born into the family of God, through faith in God's Son as a personal Saviour. This is the first step. There follows a nurturing and a growth, the rate of which is roughly proportional to the regularity and eagerness with which one feeds on God's word, prays, and commits his ways unto God. A completely committed man may, in very short time, become a spiritual giant. Conversely, the man of little faith may remain a comparable weakling, or runt, though nevertheless a member of the family into which he has been born by faith in Jesus Christ. Such a one is not to be censored by his fellow Christians, but rather to be upheld in prayer and helped with his burdens.

The requirements for spiritual growth and fitness that follow the new birth therefore are quite analagous to those for physical growth and fitness in the wake of physical birth—proper diet and proper exercise. The Christian must feed on the Word and keep out of his diet harmful and/or toxic substances, such as lewd literature, shady conversation and thoughts, lust-filled leisure. His spiritual exercise must consist of prayer, witnessing, and walking in the Spirit; and the more he exercises, the tougher and more enduring will be his spiritual muscles.

I was born into the family of God many years ago, while yet a teenager, when I accepted Christ at his word and realized that even though I had never committed any horrendous crime I was, in the eyes of God and by inherent nature, a sinner unfit for his kingdom. Christ saved me, and for a time I grew by leaps and bounds in my spiritual experience.

But Satan never rests. A few years after my experience he made the grass appear greener in another pasture, into which I strayed from my Shepherd's flock. But thanks be to his eternal grace, he loved me enough to call me back just a few years ago, and that by way of a crazy EKG. Thus what seemed so terrible and black at the time I praise now as an act of my Saviour's love. God sent the threat of physical heart disease into my life to point out a much more serious disease of the heart—the disease of sin! For while physical heart disease may claim this body, thanks be to my God's unceasing love it can never claim my eternal spirit, for that belongs eternally to my eternal God, who bought it with the blood of Christ.

A before and after comparison of spiritual fitness parameters might, in my own case, look something like this:

|                            | *Before*   | *After*        |
|----------------------------|------------|----------------|
| Prayer Life                | Nil        | Daily          |
| Bible reading              | Rarely     | Regularly      |
| Bible memory               | Rarely     | Regularly      |
| Church attendance          | Rarely     | Regularly      |
| Christian fellowship       | Undesired  | Highly desired |
| Spiritual awareness in daily living | Absent | Very present |

As a Christian, I am more aware of my shortcomings and failures than anyone. When I think of how miserably I have failed my Lord in the past, and how I still come up wanting, I can only wonder the more at his supernal love, and strive the harder to keep him at the center of all I do. Whatever I may do to his glory is by his grace and power, and not mine. For I am one of the spiritually weak. Yet my God is great and merciful, and he knows the inner longings of my heart. He will never fail, which is basically how I came to cross the bridge.

**CHAPTER X**

# Of Other Bridges

I am the way, the truth, and the life:
no man cometh unto the Father, but by me.
Christ Jesus (John 14:6)

I am well aware that faith of the so-called religious variety is considered by the unbeliever to be a sign of weakness, and that many an erudite psychologist would rear back in his professorial chair and pronounce my use of it as but one of any number of bridges which might be used by different persons in similar situations. Other bridges might be faith in a medical or a surgical procedure (of which I am by no means totally devoid), or in a fellow being, such as a physician (also in which, as a whole, I have great confidence), or simply in a set of cold, bare facts, so-called, such as these which I dug out of the library.

Many would ask: Is not fear but an expression of inferiority, in the first place, and is not Bible-based faith but an illusion to salve the troubled heart? If the first of these tenets be true, we are all inferior beings differing only in degree, for every living creature possesses a built-in instinctual response to a threatening or hostile force. If the last be true, then we brand God a liar, for he tells us that "without faith it is impossible to please him," and that his Word is the only absolute Rock in an otherwise perishing creation.

As a matter of fact, the Christian faith is the perfect antidote for fear. Fear cannot exist in its true presence, certainly not as a permanent and paralyzing emotion, as it was before I took God at his word. And vice versa: Faith in the one true God cannot exist alongside a dominating fear. Else how could Paul and Silas have sung so staunchly while prisoners in a Roman cell? Or how could Peter have gone so willingly to his inverse crucifixion in defense of his Lord? Or how could Stephen have succumbed with a prayer for others on his lips while stones beat the life slowly from him? Or how could thousands of early martyrs die by fire and sword, or in Roman arenas by teeth and claw, rather than deny the blood that bought them? Here was faith at its triumphant best over fear.

Yet the ultimate test of one's faith is not the believer, but rather the object of his belief. For you see, kamikaze pilots have slammed their planes into carrier decks with no concern whatever for their lives—because of faith in a symbol. Black men have spilled their blood on African soil for centuries because of faith in heathen gods living, they supposed, in a string of bones about their necks. Brown skins have parched and withered into nothingness for worship of serpents or cows. And yellow-skinned men have dared torture and death to please a god preserved in wood, as helpless and mute in his carved imagery as he was in life itself. Thus do Christian and Buddhist and Hindu or heathen have one thing in common—a faith.

But the burning question is what—nay, *who*—is the object of that faith? What does that faith guarantee? Does its existence depend on a believer, or can it stand alone? Who stands behind it? Who validates it? Who makes it *live?* Does its Originator claim to be Alpha and Omega, and can he prove it? Has he *already* proved it? Does his Word bear clear testimony, by way of a Person who lived sinlessly, died fearlessly, and rose again just as had been predicted thousands of years before, that he is eternal and can and will freely bestow on whosoever will come unto him eternal life? Does the object of your faith have all the answers to the imponderables that are the grass roots of life? If so, it is a perfect bridge.

You see, friend, if all one has on which to hang his hat is some man-made philosophy, he does indeed have much to fear. On the other hand, if one be of the household of the one true God, fear has no dominion over him, for perfect love (which is God) casteth out fear. Bridges other than faith in Christ—a very personal faith

—must sooner or later fail you, for they are built on the shifting sands of imperfection.

No thinking man can long ignore the kaleidoscopic parade of heights and depths which demarcate the drama called life: its valleys and its mountains; birth and demise; health and disease; beginning and ending; sunrise and sunset; triumph and tragedy; life and death. What indeed, is life?

What is death? What is truth? What is real and what is fiction? When blow the cold and chilling monsoons that crash, sooner or later, into every life, most of us somewhere along the line form philosophies of one sort or another—philosophies designed to tide us over the rough spots of life, to give answers which afford some sort of consolation, whether they be based on seeming truth or on fancy. But philosophies born of man are doomed to fall short. Witness the psychiatric hospitals and psychiatrists' offices, filled to overflowing. Witness the self-destruction. Witness the escape routes—alchohol, drugs, death-defying acts of bravado. Witness soaring divorce rates. Witness the flaunting of law and order and of justice. Witness wars and rumours of war. Witness unhappiness, despair, gloom, dissatisfaction, emptiness, and a thousand-and-one other evidences that the answer to such perplexing and mind-boggling questions cannot evolve from the mind of man. For man, bogged down in a more of confusion, lost in a maze of uncertainty, is incapable of pulling himself up by his own bootstraps, mentally or otherwise.

For many years I searched for the answers to such questions. I am happy to say that I found them. Not in some textbook or at the foot of some human fount of knowledge, and certainly not from any tapestry of wisdom woven of my own disparaging thoughts. I found truth in the Man who said: "I am the way, the truth, and the life." I found truth in the Man Christ Jesus, Son of the living God!

Such Truth does not depend on man, for it existed before ever the earth was flung into space. It stands on its own, alone. This Truth was God incarnate; was "in the beginning with God"; is "from everlasting to everlasting"; and is "without whom was not anything made that was made."

When I accepted Christ as my personal Saviour, then Truth became a part of me, and I a part of Truth. Where there had been perplexity there now was clarity. Where there had been uncertainty there now was assurance. Where there had been anxiety there now was "peace that passeth understanding."

Truth is not manufactured by a philosophy, nor philosophies by truth. Nobel prize-winner Francis Crick had this to say: "To those of you who may be vitalists I would make this prophecy: What everyone believed yesterday and you believe today, only cranks will believe tomorrow." Truth, total truth, is a verity beyond the comprehension of the human mind.

Said the Man Christ Jesus: "I am . . . the truth." Life, eternal life, is a grail for which man has searched, fruitlessly, since the beginning of time.

Said the One for whom and by whom all things were made: "I am . . . the life." No mere man has ever posed the questions, supplied the answers, flung the gauntlet, and conquered life and death as did the Man Christ Jesus. He is either a dead lie or the Living Truth; he either was the greatest con artist of all time or, verily, he was the Son of God.

How can I prove in a test-tube or by some formula that he was who he claimed to be? I cannot. And if I could, or if anyone could, he would not be God. As a famous contemporary physician (Irvine H. Page, MD) has pointed out: "The human mind operates by finite concepts which make it incapable of apprehending God. 'Either God is a Mystery or he is nothing at all.' "

Indeed, it is as the old proverb has stated: *"Dien difini est Dien finis"*—if God is defined he is finished. So we are left with an insoluble paradox whose very proof lies couched in its unfathomable mystery. That is where faith comes in, the kind of faith he commands us to have, the faith of a little child. Why? Because our childlike minds are too finite, too incapable, too limited, to comprehend total Truth—the infinite, unbelievable, illimitable greatness, wisdom, power, and love that is God. That is why we must take him on faith. Were anything more required, alas, no man could touch the hem of his garment.

Once the step of faith is taken, once he is taken at his word, the answers to all the ponderous questions fall neatly into place, like the pieces of a jig-saw puzzle. Mysteries remain, to be sure. But the answers are known to God. And to know him who knows the answers is enough for now. One Way. One Perfect Love. One Bridge.

CHAPTER XI

# Postlude

For God hath not given us the spirit of fear;
But of power, and of love, and of a sound mind.
                                    —Paul (2 Timothy 1:7)

Man's most precious physical possessions are life and health, in that order. Fear of the loss of either is his greatest fear in the same order. Tell a wealthy man he is going to die, and all his treasures become as vain baubles. Tell a selfish man he is going to lose his health, and the purse strings grow slack. Tell a prude that his days are numbered, and his vanity goes down the drain. Tell a ravishing beauty that she has an ailment that will slowly wither her away, and life no longer has any meaning.

Death and illness-unto-death are like magic wands that reduce the mighty general to the rank of buck private, that lay the white shirted and the blue denimed side by side, that make even the bank accounts of pauper and king. The quest for eternal life, like the quest for perpetual motion, has gone on for eons, and it goes on still. But to all save those in Christ Jesus eternal life remains an illusion, and so shall it ever be.

The conquest of fear, so long as one is in the flesh, will never be total, for paradoxically the total conquest of fear depends upon the death of flesh. So long as the perishable flesh remains, so also will an element of fear. This is our human portion. Only God, through Jesus Christ, ever has conquered death; and only in Christ have we assurance of life beyond the grave, so that with Paul we can jeer at death: "Oh, death, where is thy sting!" But, fearful as we are of the passageway, those who rest their case in Jesus Christ

117

will find in him the courage to go through that last door.

Yes, life indeed is a fragile thing, "even a vapour"; "grass that withereth"; but a "handbreadth" in the eyes of God. This being the case, then, and if there be such a thing as eternal life, the wise man will see to his spiritual state first, and to his physical second. Indeed, we are told in Scripture that if we seek *first* for the kingdom of God and his righteousness, all things will be added unto us.

The greatest lesson that has been taught me over the past several years is that it is far better to be spiritually healthy and physically ill than vice versa. And the corollary certainly is true: 'Tis far, far better to be physically dead and spiritually alive than spiritually dead and physically alive.

Dedicated Christians have, down through the ages, literally sacrificed their bodies to fire, sword, and cross; to starvation, imprisonment, and wild beasts; and gladly, for the cause of Christ. What the spiritually oriented man discerns is that this physical life is but a speck of sand on an ocean beach of eternity, and thus does he come to put it in its proper perspective.

Veritable spiritual giants have lived in pitifully diseased and woefully deformed bodies. God does not require that his children be able to run two miles in fifteen minutes. Sonship with God requires only recognition that Christ died for one's sins, in one's stead, according to God's plan. With such recognition comes the conquest of fear that Paul had when, in a Roman prison and faced with a certain Roman death, he could sing and proclaim triumphantly: For I know whom I have believed, and am persuaded that he is able to keep that which I have committed unto him against that day" (2 Tim. 1:12). There, at the foot of the cross of Jesus Christ, and there alone, is the conquest of fear; real, total, and complete.

Nevertheless, so long as we are in the flesh, the proper kind of physical fitness program (one built on endurance [aerobic] types of exercise of a rhythymic nature) has a definite place in the care of this earthly temple. "Know ye not that your body is the temple of the Holy Ghost which is in you, which ye have of God?" 1 Cor.

6:19.) God intends that we give earnest heed to take care of our temporal dwelling places, and the right kind of physical exercise, is subscribed to and intended by God himself. Briefly, in its proper perspective and in the right dimension, physical exercise has its place: to edify the earthly temple of God. But to give it the supreme place in one's life is to miss the mark, to put the cart before the horse.

Leisure-time physical fitness programs as yet have not been shown definitely to lengthen life. Perhaps they can. The answer is not yet known. It seems that they can increase one's chances of surviving a heart attack. And it seems that they can exert beneficial effects in numerous diseases other than those of the heart and blood vessels (such as tension-related psychosomatic disorders, in particular). They can certainly give to a man a measure of self-confidence, improve his general well-being and his outlook on physical life. As a means of relieving tension, physical exertion of proper dimensions is unsurpassed. Optimal physical fitness for one's own age and physical status is good, and to be strived for—but not as an end in itself.

What one must not forget is that joggers drop dead, some after many years of jogging. Fitness enthusiasts, even the most ardent of them, have heart attacks. And even with completely normal coronary arteries, men and women wind up in oxygen tents with abnormal EKG's. Physicians ofttime work wonders, but harken to the words of a famous contemporary physician: "The physician, competent, useful, a steadfast source of strength to his patient, finds when his own final illness comes that he does not have the ultimate answers and he does not necessarily have greater understanding or greater promise or greater confidence" (E. Grey Dimond).

Surgeons perform remarkable feats, but their statistics still reflect failure in terms of mortality. Sickness and death are inherent to the flesh. There is no escape. Sooner or later the most superb athlete, the fastest runner, the greatest miler, the strongest frame, must yield to an appointment with death. The sober man in his soberest moments realizes this, that his physical fitness, however good or bad it may be, can take him only so far—to the brink of the grave. Physical fitness may be a balm for many earthly ills, and I thank God that he chose it as an instrument for refinement of my own sorely tried body and soul, but it is not a panacea, and most assuredly it is not the fountain of eternal life.

Dear reader, the problems you have in life doubtless are not mine at all, for one's troubles are as individual as one's fingerprints. Yours may be frustration, loneliness, despair, futility, hopelessness; yours may be financial, social, personal, business; yours may be any of a thousand and one things. It may be that you have a problem that can be shared with no one except God. But whatever your need, I assure you that God can meet it, *if you are in Christ!* How do I know? He met mine, and he meets it still.

But without Christ, our Mediator with God, there simply is no hope for the best of us in the best of circumstances. Contrariwise, with him, there is every hope for the worst of us in the worst of circumstances.

Are you in the grip of some dread disease? Do you lie on a sick bed or, perhaps worse, on a death bed? Are you in such dire straits—physical, financial, family, or otherwise—that there seems to be no hope at all? Dear friend, let me assure that Jesus Christ is the answer. There is no problem for which he does not have an answer, no situation beyond his solution.

This book could well be entitled: "The Conquest of Fear through Faith." For physical fitness, what measure of it God has given me, has been with me a product of faith, but an incidental tool that my Lord has used to bring me closer to him. How long it shall please him to let me continue here I do not know. But the important thing is that no longer am I filled with fear. Each time I run, each time I feel the joy of muscles in action, I thank him for the lesson of these past few years. And I know that through this physical experience he has molded me just a little more in the image of Christ, in whose likeness someday I shall be perfected, as will every believer.

If there is something in your life beyond your comprehension, physical or otherwise, take it to Jesus. You will be amazed at how he will use it to fashion you, also. How can I be so sure? If he could conquer the fears of a man like myself, he can do it for you also. And the beauty of it is that he will! Just ask! Won't you try it and see? You will never regret it!

In summary, it is perfect love, the love of God for you and me through Jesus Christ, that conquers fear. I recommend this love to you. Whatever your fear, it will die at the foot of Christ's cross, God's expression of perfect love!

*There is no fear in love; but perfect love casteth out fear* (1 Jno. 4:18).

*For God hath not given us the spirit of fear; but of power, and of love, and of a sound mind* (2 Tim. 1:7).

# *Bibliography*

## Books

1. Graham, M. F. *Prescription for life* (New York: David McKay Co., Inc.), 1966.
2. *A National Program to Conquer Heart Disease, Cancer, and Stroke* Vol. I, Dec. 1964, U. S. Government Printing Office. [See additional listings after chapters 3, 4, and 7.]

## Periodicals

1. *American Journal of Cardiology*
Holloszy, J.; Skinner, James; Toro, G.; and Cureton, Thomas, "Effects of a Six-month Program of Endurance Exercise on the Serum Lipids of Middle-Aged Men," Vol. 14, 1964.
2. *American Journal of Clinical Nutrition*
Monteye, H. J.; Van Huse, W. D.; Brewer, W. D.; Jones, E. M.; *et al,* "Effect of Exercise on Blood Cholesterol in Middle-Aged Men," Mar-Apr, 1959.
3. *Annals of Internal Medicine*
Groom, D., McKee, E. E., *et al,* "Development Patterns of Coronary and Aortic Atherosclerosis in Young Negroes of Haiti and the United States," Nov., 1964.
4. *Annals of Thoracic Surgery*
Adam, Maurice, "Immediate Revascularization of the Ischemic Heart," 9: 297–300, 1970.
5. *British Heart Journal*
Stamler, J., "Acute Myocardial Infarction. Prognosis in Primary Prevention," 1971, 33, Supplement.
6. *Bulletin of the American Heart Association*
Report of the Committee on Nutrition of the American Heart Association, Summer, 1965, "Diet and Heart Disease." By permission of the American Heart Association, Inc.
7. *Circulation*
Bierenbaum, *et al,* "Five-Year Experience of Modified Fat Diets on Younger Men with Coronary Heart Disease," Nov., 1970.

Rechnitzer, P., *et al,* "Long-Term Follow-Up Study of Survival and Recurrence Rates Following Myocardial Infarction in Exercising and Control Subjects," April, 1972.

Strong, J. P.; Tejada-V, Carlos; McGill, J. C., Jr.; and Holman, R. L., "Comparison of Early Lesions of Atherosclerosis in New Orleans, Guatemala, and Costa Rica," Sept., 1957.

8. *Circulation Research*

Eckstein, R. W., "Effect of Exercise and Coronary Artery Narrowing on Coronary Collateral Circulation," Vol. 5, 1967.

9. *Consultant*

White, Paul D., "Recognizing the Candidate for Coronary Heart Disease," Feb., 1965 (Smith, Kline, and French Laboratories).

10. *The Heart Bulletin*

Katz, L. N., and Pick, Ruth, "Hypercholesterolemia and Heart Disease," Sept-Oct, 1959. Copyrighted by the Medical Arts Publishing Foundation.

11. *Hospital Medicine*

Boyer, John L., "Physical Activity Program Following Myocardial Infarction," Mar., 1972.

12. *Hospital Practice*

Hellerstein, H. K., "Rehabilitation of the Postinfarction Patient," July, 1972.

Stamler, J., "The Primary Prevention of Coronary Heart Disease," Sept., 1971.

13. *Journal of the American Medical Association*

Enos, William F.; Beyer, James C.; and Holmes, Robert H., "Pathogenesis of Coronary Disease in American Soldiers Killed in Korea," July 16, 1955.

Luongo, E. P., "Health Habits and Heart Disease . . ." Nov. 10, 1956.

Ziegler, E., "Relation Between Cardiovascular Mortality and Sugar Consumption in Switzerland," abstracted from Praxis 60:1971, May 10, 1971.

"Prevention of Coronary Heart Disease: The Fat's in the Fire," editorial, Sept. 17, 1965.

"Fasting May Have Undesirable Results," report on work of Benoit, F. L., April 5, 1965.

14. *Journal of Sports Medical and Physical Fitness*

Burt, John J., and Jackson, R., "The Effects of Physical Exercise on the Coronary Collateral Circulation of Dogs," Vol. 5, 1965.

15. *Journal of Thoracic Cardiovascular Surgery*

Mitchel, Ben F., "Ascending Aorta-to-Coronary Artery Saphenous Vein By-pass Grafts," 60:457–67, October, 1970.

16. *Medical Science*

"Coronary Artery Disease," April 25, 1957 (J. B. Lippincott Co.).

17. *Medical Tribune*

Fejfar, Zdenek, "The Heart of Medicine and the Heart of Man," guest editorial, Oct. 25, 1972.

Glenn, William L., "Heart Experts Assail 'Enthusiastic' Surgery," Dec. 8, 1971.

Harrison, R., "Exercise Lowers Cholesterol in Laboratory Animal Tests," Dec. 2, 1964.

Raab, W., "Why Heart Reconditioning Centers?" Dec. 23, 1964.

American Heart Association Annual Report (1964), reported in "Medicine in the Public View," Mar. 8, 1965. By permission of the American Heart Association, Inc.

"Exercise: Its Therapeutic Value Was Known to Plato," Dec. 23, 1964.

"Fitness Program Held Beneficial," Mar. 8, 1965.

"Six-Month Exercising Course Assists Postinfarct Patients," Nov. 17, 1971.

Survey of Trends. From a Study by the American Heart Association, the Public Health Service, and the National Heart Institute, Mar. 13–14, 1965.

18. *Medical World News*

Stamler, J., "An Interview: Heading Off Heart Disease," Sept. 17, 1965.

"Late News: Starvation Dieters Lose Weight but not Fat," May 14, 1965.

"Medical Achievements: Diet Against Heart Disease," Jan. 15, 1965.

"Sugar: Dangerous to the Heart?" Feb. 12, 1971.

19. *Minnesota Medicine*

Hellerstein, H. K., "The Effects of Physical Activity," Aug., 1969.

Oglesby, Paul, "Physical Inactivity," Aug., 1969.

20. *Modern Concepts of Cardiovascular Disease*

Fox, Sam M.; Naughton, John P.; and Gorman, Patrick A., "Physical Activity and Cardiovascular Health. 1. Potential for Prevention of Coronary Heart Disease and ossible Mechanisms," April, 1972.

21. *Modern Medicine*

Page, I., and Hilleboe, H., "Atherosclerosis and Coronary Heart Disease; An Interview," Dec. 1, 1957.

Page, I. H., "Diet and Exercise for Prevention of Atherosclerosis—Both or Neither?" July 12, 1971.

Van Itallie, T. B., and Hashim, S. A., "Obesity in an Age of Caloric Anxiety," Nov. 30, 1970.

(re- Hellerstein, H. K.), "Contemporaries," Oct. 19 1970.

22. *New England Journal of Medicine*

Mann, G. V.; Teel, K.; *et al*, "Exercise in the Disposition of Dietary Calories," Vol. 253, 1955.

23. *Parade,* Nov. 28, 1965.

24. *Physical Fitness Research Digest.* President's Council on Physical Fitness and Sports. Series 2, no. 2, April, 1972.

25. *Texas State Journal of Medicine*

Stare; Fred J., "Nutrition in Cardiovascular Diseases," 61:111–14, Feb., 1965.

**All quotes used by permission.**